A Time of Fulfillment

A Time of Fulfillment

Spiritual Reflections for
Advent and Christmas

Anselm Grün, OSB

Translated by Mark Thamert, OSB

LITURGICAL PRESS
Collegeville, Minnesota

www.litpress.org

Cover design by Stefan Killen. Cover photos © ThinkStock and iStockphoto.

Originally published in 2012 as *Zeit der Erfüllung: Ein Begleiter für Advent und Weihnachten* © Vier-Türme GmbH, Verlag, D-97359 Münsterschwarzach Abtei.

1	2	3	4	5	6	7	8	9

Library of Congress Cataloging-in-Publication Data

Grün, Anselm.
    [Zeit der Erfüllung. English]
    A time of fulfillment : spiritual reflections for Advent and Christmas / Anselm Grün ; translated by Mark Thamert.
       pages   cm
    ISBN 978-0-8146-3809-5 — ISBN 978-0-8146-3834-7 (ebook)
     1. Advent—Meditations.   2. Christmas—Meditations.
I. Title.

BV40.G7813   2013
242'.33—dc23
                                     2013015172

Contents

Preface

Advent and Christmas invite us to reflect in new ways upon the mystery of this season. During these weeks many people feel a deep yearning to celebrate the feast so that it touches and transforms them. At the same time, they are incapable of understanding the mysteries of this season and of implementing them in their lives. People long for quiet but are unable to find peace. They want to be moved by Advent and Christmas songs, but the texts and melodies remain superficial. They would like to hear the liturgical texts in such a way that they might touch their hearts. But the words pass them by.

So I would like to offer help in this book so that readers might experience Advent more intensively and understand the mystery of Christmas better. The book that follows has two parts: one for Advent and one for Christmas.

For Advent I have decided to focus on the O-Antiphons. These antiphons, for the last seven days of Advent before Christmas Eve, continue to move me year after year. I have meditated on them, so that you, dear reader, might understand these wonderful ancient texts and intuit in them the mystery of Advent. In the process I have focused on two antiphons for each week of Advent and have given concrete suggestions how, with rituals and exercises, you might implement the messages of the antiphons in your own life.

For the feast of Christmas I have tried to interpret the biblical texts that deal with Christmas. We hear these texts at Christmas time, but sometimes they remain foreign or distant. So it is good to consult these biblical texts for their claims about Christmas. This will take us not only through the three gospels that deal with Christmas—Matthew, Luke and John, but I will also take a look at the messages of the Letter of Titus and in the Letter to the Hebrews, the biblical letters we read at Christmas, a time when many people have the chance to read. So it is meaningful to read and meditate on the texts we have heard during the Christmas season to grasp more fully their true messages.

I wish you, dear reader, a blessed Advent and Christmas season. I hope that these texts move you and bring Christ into your heart, so that he might be born in you, and renew, illuminate, and heal your life.

Anselm Grün, OSB

PART 1
Advent Season

The Message of the O-Antiphons

The O-Antiphons

Imagining Christ in Song

From the seventh century the O-Antiphons have been sung at Vespers (Evening Prayer) during the last seven days before Christmas. They all begin with the salutation, "O."

The O-Antiphons, sung before Mary's song of praise (the *Magnificat*), are songs full of yearning. In them we celebrate mysterious images in song. For centuries these antiphons have touched the hearts of monks, as well as others who have immersed themselves in the wonderful words and melodies.

The O-Antiphons describe God, using various traits and images taken from the Old Testament. At first these images referred only to God, but they were applied to Jesus Christ from the beginning of the antiphon tradition. They say something about the mystery of God but also about the mystery of Jesus Christ. In the O-Antiphons the art of interpreting Old Testament text as images for the coming of Jesus Christ into the world becomes apparent. We also see how the mystery of salvation in Jesus Christ has been made visible in these old images.

Images open windows through which we can see realities formerly hidden from us. Images want to infuse themselves into us and to change us from the inside out. The images of the O-Antiphons, as Meister Eckhart, the late medieval mystic, once said, are meant to impress Christ within us so that we may also express Christ, so that Christ may become audible and visible in this world through our thoughts, speech, and actions.

These images reveal to us the mystery of God and of his incarnate Son. The O-Antiphons also describe God's actions with words and images of the Old Testament.

Each O-Antiphon closes with the plea, "Come." With this appeal for the coming of God in Jesus Christ, the antiphon includes one of seven requests that correspond to seven ancient human longings. If God comes in the person of Jesus Christ, then God will free, save, heal, and illuminate us. We ask that God accomplish in us everything we long for in the depths of our souls.

The O-Antiphons are sung in a special way. They are heard in the second mode, which in the tradition is the mode of young women. Here it is the tone of longing, which takes the singer to the extreme and then concludes with an inner call for the coming of the Lord.

The cantor in our Münsterschwarzach Abbey who had taught me Gregorian chant in the novitiate once told us that the first monks of the abbey (reestablished in 1913) did not have much of a sense of the details of chant. They had to devote themselves first of all to the external building needs of the abbey. But they sang the O-Antiphons of the last days of Advent with a special fervor. They conveyed the idea to the young monks of the time that these antiphons should be sung slowly and solemnly.

Today the great bell of the abbey church rings during the O-Antiphons in order to announce the mystery of these songs. These O-Antiphons are sung in a special order. On the 17th of December the abbot intones the first antiphon, on the 18th the prior intones the second, and then the oldest confrere, and the next oldest, and so on. It is an honor to intone these antiphons. Vespers are celebrated on these days with liturgical vestments. During the *Magnificat* the altar is incensed.

Each year I feel how mysteriously the O-Antiphons move me. They touch my Advent longing. The meaning of Advent is given expression in them. So in this book I would like to reflect on the O-Antiphons, first for myself so that I can sing them more consciously and understand them more deeply. But I would also like to consider them in such a way that you, dear readers, may feel addressed and may experience in these words the mystery of Advent.

The O-Antiphons are sung from the 17th to the 23rd of December. I want to elucidate them in such a way that they may accompany us and clarify the meaning of Advent during the entire season. For this reason I would like to reflect on two antiphons for each of the first three weeks and one antiphon for the final week. The texts and images can then guide us and open to us the mystery of Advent each week, which closes then with suggestions for the week.

There are seven O-Antiphons. The liturgy loves the number seven. There are seven sacraments, seven gifts of the Holy Spirit, seven consolations, and seven days of the week. Seven is the number of transformation. Thus is hidden in the number seven of the O-Antiphons a kind of longing that our lives will be transformed by the coming of Jesus Christ and that we will be penetrated more and more by his spirit. Human transformation brought about by the seven sacraments should also be brought about by the O-Antiphons. Singing the mystery-filled words and images allows the image of Jesus Christ, our Redeemer and Savior, to be implanted in us ever more deeply.

Advent season is characterized not only by the desire and appeal that Jesus might come again once and for all, to call the whole world back into his kingdom and to bring about the end of the world. More importantly it has to do with the desire that Jesus come to us here and now in order to enter into us and to fill us with his spirit.

Singing the O-Antiphons creates the concrete place where Christ knocks at the door of our hearts in order to find entrance into us. In our singing he comes to us. When we sing these antiphons we need not believe everything we sing, but, in our singing, faith takes shape. In our singing, Christ fills us. All we need to do is to let him in. Reflecting on the words and images prepares us to let Christ himself enter into us.

Advent points toward the arrival of Christ—at every moment. But it also means the ultimate return of Christ. However, this ultimate arrival happens not at the end of the world, but in the death of each individual. In death the world comes to an end for us. In death Jesus comes to us in an ultimate way in order to permeate and transform us forever with his spirit. He wants to transform us once and for all into that unique image that God has made for each of us.

In our singing of the O-Antiphons, something of this transformation is already taking place, as images of Jesus Christ are built up within us and "build" us; they form and shape us more and more in the image of Jesus Christ.

The Church Fathers interpreted the word from the Book of Genesis in this way:

> Then God said, "Let us make humankind in our image, according to our likeness." (Gen 1:26)

We are all an image, an icon, of God. It is our task to become ever more like this unique image of God. If we do, we will become the persons God himself imagined.

Our singing of the images of Christ in the O-Antiphons allows them to implant themselves ever more deeply in us so that we become more and more like the image of Christ and the unique image of God in each of us.

A Weekly Ritual during the Advent Season

In many families it is a tradition on Saturday evening —the vigil of each Sunday of Advent—to sit down around the Advent wreath, to light the appropriate candles, and to sing an Advent song. A good ritual for the Advent season would be to combine the lighting of the candles on the Advent wreath with a reading—or, if possible, the singing—of an O-Antiphon.

The symbolism of the Advent wreath is grasped in spoken images in the O-Antiphons. It is good to first of all reflect on the meaning of the Advent wreath before we turn to the O-Antiphons. The Advent wreath is not only an external decoration. In it a deeper meaning lies hidden.

In antiquity the wreath was a crown of victory. The Advent wreath promises that our lives will be successful. The round form of the wreath shows that our inner brokenness will be mended and that our sharp and brittle parts will be smoothed out. The wreath is also the promise that the family, which sometimes threatens to fall apart, will now reunite around the candles we light on the Advent wreath. This light now shines within us all.

The Bible speaks often about the wreath. I would like to limit myself to a few New Testament verses. Saint Paul, for example, compares our lives with that of an athlete who lives a life of abstinence in order to obtain the victory wreath:

> Athletes exercise self-control in all things; they do it to receive a perishable wreath, but we an imperishable one. (1 Cor 9:25)

The Advent wreath refers to the victory wreath (crown), which does not wither through death, but rather remains eternal, because God himself places it on our heads.

The Second Letter of Timothy takes up this image:

> From now on there is reserved for me the crown of righteousness, which the Lord, the righteous judge, will give me on that day, and not only to me but also to all who have longed for his appearing. (2 Tim 4:8)

This is an Advent text. During Advent we all wait for the appearance of Jesus Christ—not only at the end of the world, but also here and now. When Jesus enters my heart, he crowns me with the wreath of righteousness; everything in me is set right, everything becomes right and just. Thus I become just in my very being, and I can live honestly and genuinely.

Also, the message of the First Letter of Peter to his readers sounds like an Advent promise:

> And when the chief shepherd appears, you will win the crown of glory that never fades away. (1 Pet 5:4)

The Advent wreath makes us aware of the coming of Jesus. In the death of every person it is not anxiety that meets us, but rather the chief shepherd, the shepherd who has already led us to green pastures. It is the Good Shepherd, Jesus Christ himself. And he will crown us with a wreath of glory that will not fade. Not only a wreath of justice but also of glory, it shows us the beauty of the original image in which God has made each of us. Its glory will not be taken away from us in death but instead will shine in its true radiance.

The Letter of James places the wreath into our everyday lives. It will protect us. The wreath is the promise that we will not lose ourselves in the hazards of daily life but rather stand firm:

> Blessed is anyone who endures temptation. Such a one has stood the test and will receive the crown of life that the Lord has promised to those who love him. (Jas 1:12)

The wreath of life has already been promised to us—under the condition that we stand firm and love God in our daily lives. The one who loves God has already received the crown of life and he experiences what true life is like—it is happier than the life of those who shine only outwardly. The image of the wreath also appears often in the Book of Revelation. The Seer urges us to be true until death:

> I will give you the crown of life. (Rev 2:10)

The 24 elders who stand before the throne of God wear golden wreaths on their heads. (cf. Revelation 4:4) They symbolize to us the glory that awaits us in death. The wreath refers to Mary and to Jesus. The liturgy has interpreted this passage in Revelation as referring to Mary:

> A great portent appeared in heaven: a woman clothed with the sun, with the moon under her feet, and on her head a crown of twelve stars. (Rev 12:1)

This description refers also to us when we, in faith, like Mary, come to depend completely on God.

Jesus himself wears a golden crown:

> Then I looked, and there was a white cloud, and seated
> on the cloud was one like the Son of Man, with a golden
> crown on his head, and a sharp sickle in his hand! (Rev
> 14:14)

When Christ lives in us—when we receive Christ at
communion or when we imagine in our meditations
that he is within us—we wear a golden crown with him.
This crown makes clear that no one rules over us, but
instead we have become truly free in Christ. Examining
the Advent wreath in the light of these biblical texts can
strengthen our faith. In faith we are already wearing a
crown. In faith we trust that we will overcome obstacles
in life and that our coming together as a family will be
blessed.

On Saturday evening—on the vigil of each Advent
Sunday—one more candle is lit on the Advent wreath.
When this happens we should reflect on the symbolism
of the different candles, each of which has its own meaning:

The *first candle* expresses our longing for unity. I
yearn to be one with myself, content with my life story,
but also to be one with God.

The *second candle* refers to a polarity—between man
and woman, between young and old, or between light
and darkness. All opposites within me will be illuminated; the conflicts within our families will also be filled
with light. These opposites will not lead to discord as

they do in many families. When all polarities are filled with light, they strengthen the light for us all.

The *third candle* symbolizes a kind of trinity. We have within, three parts: body, soul and spirit—or head, heart and belly. All three parts are to be illuminated by the light of Christ. Thus the promise is fulfilled that Jesus gave in the Gospel of Luke:

> "If then your whole body is full of light, with no part of it in darkness, it will be as full of light as when a lamp gives you light with its rays." (Luke 11:36)

We ourselves become light for others.

The *fourth candle* refers to earthly things and every-day life. Four stands for the four elements and thus for things of the earth, the world and everyday life. Our daily lives and their mundane activities are to be filled with the light of Christ. When our daily life reflects the light of Christ, the light in our house will become brighter. Everything will gradually be illuminated by his light.

That is the promise of the Advent wreath, until we celebrate the light at Christmas that shines forth from the child in the manger.

The evangelist John says:

> The true light, which enlightens everyone, was coming into the world. . . . And the Word became flesh and lived among us, and we have seen his glory, the glory as of a father's only son, full of grace and truth. (John 1:9, 14)

The Advent wreath and its four candles express what will be developed in the images of the seven O-Antiphons. I would like then to connect the interpretation of the O-Antiphons with each of the respective weeks of Advent.

First Week of Advent

The first week of Advent has to do with the movement from busyness to peace. If we want to celebrate the arrival of Jesus, we must first of all arrive at home within ourselves. We must—as the first candle makes clear—become one with ourselves and find harmony within ourselves. Only then are we able to become one with Christ.

Advent is the time of our arrival within, of coming to peace and of reaching our center. If we have arrived within ourselves, then the word of God can also arrive to touch our hearts.

The first two antiphons describe this coming of God in Jesus Christ as revelation and liberation. They address important longings that arise within us whenever we try to become quiet.

In quiet, things become clearer to us. We yearn for inner freedom. We ourselves will begin to live instead of our lives being lived for us.

O Sapientia—O Wisdom

> O Sapiéntia, quæ ex ore Altíssimi prodísti, attíngens a fine usque ad finem, fórtiter suavitérque dispónens ómnia: veni ad docéndum nos viam prudéntiæ.

> O Wisdom, you came forth from the mouth of the Most High, and reaching from the beginning to end, you ordered all things mightily and sweetly: Come, and teach us the way of prudence.

The Old Testament understands wisdom as something that issues forth from God. Wisdom itself is God and, at the same time, that which comes from God and streams out toward God's people. Often it is represented as an independent force, or even as a person.

In the prologue to his gospel, John the Evangelist answers the older Wisdom texts with his discourse about the word of God:

> In the beginning was the Word, and the Word was with God, and the Word was God. (John 1:1)

In a similar way, in the Book of Proverbs, wisdom speaks of itself:

> The LORD created me at the beginning of his work, the first of his acts of long ago. Ages ago I was set up, at the first, before the beginning of the earth. (Prov 8:22-23)

Everything has come about through the wisdom of God. Already in the beginning it was with God. And God himself is wisdom.

The Book of Sirach expresses it in a similar way. Both books—the Book of Proverbs and the Book of Sirach—are Wisdom Books. They have joined the wisdom of Israel with the wisdom of Greece and Egypt and have collected sayings that summarize the wisdom of the peoples. In both books wisdom is seen as a person who emanates from God. This is what wisdom says in the Book of Sirach:

> "I came forth from the mouth of the Most High, and covered the earth like a mist. I dwelt in the highest heavens, and my throne was in a pillar of cloud. Alone I compassed the vault of heaven and traversed the depths of the abyss." (Sir 24:3-5)

The first O-Antiphon refers to these scripture texts when it says, "O Wisdom, coming forth from the mouth of the Most High." Wisdom is from God and is God. The antiphon relates wisdom to Jesus Christ. In him the wisdom of God is concentrated. He has become wisdom for us. Paul speaks of the wisdom of the cross that undermines the wisdom of the world. For those who believe,

> Christ [is] the power of God and the wisdom of God. (1 Cor 1:24)

Jesus fulfills our longing to be wise. Jesus is the wisdom of God become man. When we look to him, we see more deeply: We understand our own lives and we understand deeper connections in the world.

The first O-Antiphon describes this wisdom: "You reach from one end of the world to the other, in power and gentleness you order all things." Wisdom dwells in the whole world. Everything that has been created has been created through wisdom and permeated with wisdom. Everywhere in creation we meet the wisdom of God, realized in God's becoming human in a new way in Jesus Christ. Through wisdom God touches all of creation.

Advent is not only an event between God and humans; it also happens on a cosmic scale. When God comes to earth in his Son, the cosmos itself changes. The divine seed is planted in the earth. The earth is no longer without God. It is permeated by God's wisdom.

Not only wisdom but ultimately love too permeates all things. Teilhard de Chardin, the French Jesuit and naturalist, speaks of the "amorization" of the cosmos. In God's becoming human in Jesus Christ, God permeates the whole world. Everywhere—in people, plants, animals, in matter itself, we come into contact with this love made human.

The antiphon proclaims that wisdom, which is love, orders everything in power and gentleness. This event is brought to completion in Jesus Christ, who brings together the poles of power and gentleness. He is full of *dynamis*, full of the power of the Holy Spirit. He preaches with such a power that demons must retreat. But he orders the world and its people in gentleness as well. He treats people gently, especially broken people. He heals their wounded hearts. He surrounds them with his gentleness so that they will treat themselves gently instead of denying or judging themselves.

We yearn for Jesus to bring together power and gentleness in us. We want to emerge with power before others, to form our lives with power, to lead our company, to bring something about in our parish or in society. But we do not want to use the kind of power that will run over and suppress others. That's why power needs gentleness or mildness. The word "mild" comes from the word "to mill" and means to make fine and tender. We should live with others tenderly and affectionately, to see and work with them as precious people.

In Latin the opposites, power and gentleness, are rendered as *fortiter et suaviter*. It means powerful ordering, but also pleasant, sweet, mild, and delightful dealings with people and things. Whoever deals with others *suaviter* also awakes in them their tender and delicate sides. Whoever deals with things in this way handles them—as Benedict of Nursia demands of the cellarer— as something precious, as sacred instruments of the altar. (cf. Rule of Benedict 31:10)

Which wisdom does the Bible refer to? In this instance language can give us a clue. The Greek word for wisdom, *sophia*, means that wise people have healthy senses and that they perceive things as they are. It assumes that people do not falsify things, that they do not project their own needs into things.

The Latin word *sapientia* comes from *sapere*, which means "to taste." For Latin people that person is wise who has good taste and who tastes things as they are. Those people are wise who can taste and accept themselves, the ones who can find reconciliation within. Because they can taste themselves, a pleasant flavor also emanates from them. When we speak with them, we experience a pleasant flavor without a bitter aftertaste.

The word wisdom is related to the Latin word *vidi*, which is translated as "I have seen." Wisdom is seeing but seeing things as they are. It consists of looking more deeply and seeing things in their essence in order to see the mystery of things. Seeing in such a way is a contemplative seeing that ultimately sees God in all things.

We ask for the wisdom of God with deep yearning. The human spirit inevitably experiences darkness and bewilderment. Today we are often bewildered because we are offered so many varieties of wisdom. It is hard to find our way through all of this. We do not know whom to follow or whom to trust. We often see only superficially when we see all the facts reported to us by the media.

But how should we interpret and understand the facts? We long for God himself to come in Jesus Christ. We hope that he will reveal to us the way of wisdom and insight.

In the Latin version we ask that he teach us the way of prudence, *prudentia*. Prudence is different from wisdom. But they belong together. Prudence is the ability to decide things correctly. Amid the many spiritual and ideological recommendations that are given to us daily, we need prudence to be able to decide which path will truly lead to life.

In our translation we hear the words wisdom and insight. We yearn for God himself to come into our world and to lead us in the way of wisdom. Only when he shows us the way can we then follow him in his ways. But it also has to do with the light God has given us so that we can see more clearly. This is the only way we can have a deeper insight into the interconnectedness of the world and also of our own lives. We would like to look into the incomprehensibility of our world and the reason for our lives.

In these times when everyone speaks his opinion and declares that he has found the solution to all the problems of the world, we long for the clarity that God himself gives us. Advent is the promise that God himself—the source of all wisdom—will come to us and teach us how we should proceed on our way. Along along with the eclipse of God's image that we experience today, we yearn that God might illuminate our seeing and show us his friendly face.

In this first week of Advent, as we become quiet and arrive at peace, we will also long to see clearly and to gain a deeper insight into the mystery of our lives. We want to peer into our own souls, which we often do not understand because they are so unsettled. Our emotions change constantly because we are overcome with fear, resentment and jealousy and cannot see our way clear. Wisdom helps us to perceive the origins of these emotions and to see things more clearly.

O Adonai—O Lord

> O Adonái et Dux domus Israel, qui Móysi in igne flammæ rubi apparuisti, et ei in Sina legem dedísti: veni ad rediméndum nos in brácchio exténto.

> O Adonai and Ruler the house of Israel, you appeared to Moses in the flame of the burning bush, and on Mount Sinai gave him your law. Come, and with an outstretched arm redeem us.

The Jews had such a resistance to uttering the name of God that they used other names instead. One of the names was *Adonai*, which means "Lord." God revealed himself in the thorn bush as

> "I AM WHO I AM." (Exod 3:14)

This experience was so sacred for the Jews that they did not trust themselves to utter the name. With the name Adonai, God is seen as Lord and king over all the nations. With this name the second Antiphon calls on God. God is Lord and leader of the House of Israel. In his revealing of himself in the thorn bush God says to Moses,

> Then the LORD said, "I have observed the misery of my people who are in Egypt; I have heard their cry on account of their taskmasters. Indeed, I know their sufferings, and I have come down to deliver them from the Egyptians, and to bring them up out of that land to a good and broad land, a land flowing with milk and

> honey, to the country of the Canaanites, the Hittites, the
> Amorites, the Perizzites, the Hivites, and the Jebusites."
> (Exod 3:7-8)

Our God is a God who sees the suffering of his people.
That is the assurance of Advent: God sees our need, our
sadness and our doubt. He sees our inner taskmasters
who push us to become faster and better, to achieve
more, to become more perfect, and to look good to
everyone else. These taskmasters oppress and over-
extend us. As Lord and leader of his people, God is also
our liberator. When God rules inside of us, others stop
ruling us. We are no longer ruled by our needs and passions. When God rules inside of us we become truly
free. Christmas is the fulfillment of the promise God
made to Moses in the burning bush. At Christmas God
actually comes down to us to become one of us. At
Christmas he wants to move into our hearts in order to
rule there and to free us from all other secret rulers who
have established themselves there.

In Advent we acknowledge again and again that God
sees us. In one of the Vesper hymns we sing:

> Full of compassion you see your world threatened by
> ruin and death. You take on the world's misery and you
> heal what guilt has corrupted.

Because God sees us, he descends to meet us. Or as
Luke expresses in his beautiful *Benedictus*, God visits us
to give us salvation, redemption and healing. Because
of his merciful love God will visit us as a light radiating
from above (cf. Lk 1:78).

As in those times when Israel was oppressed in Egypt, God looks down to us today from above. He sees what we are suffering from, how we are not understood by those who surround us, how we reside in a foreign land, and how everything has become cold around us. Advent is a longing for God to come to us: in our foreign land, our suffering, and our cold. Then our foreign land will become a home. Together with him we will move from alienation to a place where we feel at home.

The second O-Antiphon tells of a God who appeared to Moses in the burning bush and who gave him the law on the mountain. Both are healing acts of God. In his appearance in the thorn bush God heals Moses, who had experienced himself as a failure. He had to flee into a foreign land. He had the feeling of being dried up, of living on the margin, and of being worthless. The thorn bush is an image of this worthlessness. But it is in this thorn bush that God appears to Moses—in a flame that shoots out of the bush.

Moses looks more closely:

> The bush was blazing, yet it was not consumed. (Exod 3:2)

The Church Fathers related this paradox to Mary, who gives birth to God and is not consumed. But the thorn bush is also a wonderful image for us. When God enflames us with his fire, we burn without being consumed. We remain completely human—with all our failures and weaknesses. And yet in God's becoming human we are filled with divine love. We remain weak and frail people, but we also become a place for God who wants to shine forth within us in our foreign land, in the homelessness we suffer as Moses did, as he shines forth in Jesus Christ.

For the Israelites, the giving of the commandments on the mountain is a healing act of God. The Israelites understood the law as a guide to freedom. God's laws were wise laws for which they were grateful. With his commandments God made it possible for the Israelites to live with one another in peace and inner and outer freedom.

With his laws God also shows us a way to succeed in life. Before God reveals the Ten Commandments to Moses he says,

> I am the LORD your God, who brought you out of the land of Egypt, out of the house of slavery. (Exod 20:2)

The commandments are the custodians of the freedom into which God led his people out of the house of bondage. God gave us commandments so that we will no longer become slaves to our own needs or to other rulers. With God's commandments we can awaken and live our lives with open eyes.

In the appeal that he come to us, we ask the God of liberation and healing, "O come and free us with your outstretched arms." All of Advent is this appeal to God that he come and free us from our entanglements. We are entangled in difficult relationships. We are caught up in the hurts of the past. We feel bound by the necessity to function in society. And we feel bound by inner fears that often load us down with senselessness—for example, the person who is afraid of driving home the same way. She believes he has to make a detour because she is afraid that otherwise something bad will happen.

Today we are burdened by many fears that take away our freedom. We ask that God free us from all these chains. And we ask that God lead us out of the land of alienation and enslavement where we are always adjusting ourselves to the expectations of others.

Advent is the time when we long for true freedom. We trust that the coming of God in the birth of his Son will lead us into this freedom.

In the Latin we hear at this point of the outstretched arm—*in brachio extento*. We ask that God stretch out his arm to free us. May he not simply watch as we fail. In Jesus Christ we ask that he show his power to us. May he appear powerfully in this world so that all people and things that have claimed power may become powerless and that we may live honest and free lives.

Suggestions

Dear reader, during the first week of Advent let these images of wisdom and the burning bush accompany you. Wisdom is the deeper knowledge of things. People have yearned for it for ages. They have wanted to see more deeply, to see through things, to see clearly, to know the origin of things. Consciously walk through the streets with the eyes of wisdom, and then listen deeply in your hearts. Is what I see true reality? Should we be occupying ourselves with hectic activity? Or is this the expression of a deeper restlessness, ultimately the restlessness Saint Augustine spoke of: "Our hearts are restless until they find rest in you, my God"?

When you walk through the countryside, try to look more deeply so that you see the wisdom of God at work in everything. Trust that everything you see has been created and formed by the word of God. The Word of God, which wants to become flesh at Christmas, enters the world in this new way in order to be the innermost cause of all things.

Take the image of the burning bush, dear reader, and meditate on it. Sit down in a comfortable chair and notice your breath and how it flows through your whole body. Then imagine: I am the burning thorn bush. I am dried up, restless, empty, disappointed by life. I am at the edge of all that is happening in the world. I am not playing a role in the world. And yet I am in the place where God's glory shines forth.

Second Week of Advent

The second week of Advent is characterized by our longing to discover and be in touch with our own roots. Many people today feel uprooted. They no longer live rooted in their ancestors or in their faith.

The rituals we practice in Advent are meant to connect us with the roots of our ancestors. For they mastered their lives with these rituals, and, with them, they also got through difficult times with trust and hope. The depressions that afflict people today have many causes, one of which is our being cut off from our roots. Those who have no roots are like a tree that is withering. When a storm comes, the tree falls.

That is why the second week of Advent invites us to reconnect with the roots of our faith—the faith of our ancestors. How did we live as children? What sustained us back then?

These questions are just as important: With what kind of rootedness did our parents, grandparents and great grandparents live? How did they experience and shape their Advent experience? What carried them in this situation? How can I participate today in the strength of their lives and faith?

The longing for one's own roots is the longing highlighted in of the second week of Advent. We also long to find access to our true selves. I want to find the key that unlocks the door to my heart, which opens the door to heaven and to other people. During the second week of Advent, we go on a hunt for the key that opens doors for us and opens our hearts to the mystery of God.

In the popular Advent song, "O Heavens Rain Down the Just One," we hear:

> For the gate was closed until our savior stepped forth.

The song depicts a heaven that has been closed. Another Advent song describes how our hearts have been closed. It challenges us to

> Open the door, fling wide the gate,
> The Lord of Glory is coming.

In the final verse of this song the one praying asks Jesus to come:

> Come, O Savior Jesus Christ
> My heart is open
> Invade my heart with your grace
> May your kindness be shown to us.

O Radix Jesse—O Root of Jesse

> O radix Iesse, qui stas in signum populórum, super quem continébunt reges os suum, quem gentes deprecabúntur: veni ad liberándum nos, iam noli tardáre.

O Root of Jesse, you stand for an ensign of humankind; before you kings shall keep silence, and to you all nations shall have recourse. Come, save us, and do not delay.

In the third O-Antiphon, Christ is addressed directly. Things focus now not on God but rather on the sprout that God calls forth from the root of Jesse. This antiphon refers to the promise of the Messiah:

A shoot shall come out from the stump of Jesse, and a branch shall grow out of his roots. The spirit of the LORD shall rest on him, the spirit of wisdom and understanding, the spirit of counsel and might, the spirit of knowledge and the fear of the LORD. (Isa 11:1-2)

We hear this promise repeatedly in the Old Testament: That God will have something new sprout from that which has been cut down, that from the ruins he will build a new city and a new temple. In this promise lies the great solace that in our time too, when we often feel cut off from the roots of the Christian tradition, God will come to us—in the person of Jesus Christ who gives us a share of God's divine root.

This promise is also an assurance that even in those instances when something in us fails, or is cut off or broken, something new can spring from what has withered. We are aware of such times of failure and brokenness. Often enough we experience an inner brokenness. We ask that the Advent season bring us to trust that, even inside of us, the tree that has been cut down may bring forth new fruit.

This promise also gives us the assurance that in our church—characterized less by blossoms today—new life may spring forth. We need not depend on ourselves alone. God himself is coming to us in Jesus Christ. Jesus is the shoot through which things, withered and cut down, are brought back into bloom. If we celebrate Christmas in the spirit of this O-Antiphon, then new life can spring up in our church even today. We should not give up hope—in spite of fewer numbers of people going to church—that our churches will be and become once again living places of the experience of God.

Coming from the root of Jesse means that Jesus has come as a sign for the nations. Jesus comes not only for individuals. As a sign to the peoples, he announces that through him something new is coming into the world and that he will change the world. When we celebrate liturgy and Christ is in our midst, we have an impact on all peoples. Then Christ becomes visible among us as sign for all peoples. He can no longer be overlooked. Christ will become visible as a sign when we publicly give witness to our faith and stand by the new hope we see for the world in Jesus Christ.

In the third Antiphon we do not hear about acts of God but rather how people react to God and Jesus Christ. "Before you the rulers of the earth are silent, the nations make their prayer." Those who rule over others are silent in the face of the power of Jesus Christ. His power is not an external power. If it were, the rulers would fight—in the belief that their means and armies were stronger. But by his silence and his radiance, Jesus silences rulers. We still have this experience today over and over. Someone wants to convince us that faith is nonsense. But then he sees a radiance in us or other believers that silences him. The arguments he wanted to proclaim get stuck in his throat.

We experienced this in the turning-point events of 1989. The people in power in East Germany would have fought against any power—and they probably would have succeeded in laying it low. But they were powerless against quietly burning candles. When they saw the candles, their cries and arguments fell silent.

When we authentically proclaim Jesus, we too will silence the rulers of the earth. Only when they are silenced can they open themselves to the message of Advent. We can also trust that in every Advent the ones who believe they have something to say will suddenly become silent and will open themselves to the mystery of the season. Advent announces that one is coming who is completely different from all the rulers of this world. Advent denotes not only a personal encounter of the individual with Jesus Christ. It also thematizes the longing for God to change our society, to silence those who shout so loudly, to make the cries of the poor audible, and to answer their cries.

When rulers fall silent, simple people have room to speak; the nations begin to entreat Jesus. When rulers become silent we are able to give words to that which really moves our hearts.

We can also understand this sentence in another way. Rulers fall silent not only before Jesus but also in our hearts. Many complain that there are always inner voices that judge and push them and do not let them experience peace. They long for quiet. But they cannot experience peace because when they are quiet the inner voices become even louder. Only when these inner voices stop plaguing us with their noise can we find the words our hearts really want to express. These are words of request, words of longing, words of entreaty that *God* might reside within us—rather than any other inner or outer power. These are petitions that God's reign may become visible in this world.

The call of the third Antiphon is one of the longest and most expressive. In it we ask Christ to come and save us, to rise up and delay no more. We place three requests before him who is to come.

That Christ may save us—that is the first plea. In our need we long for a savior. When we are about to drown in the water, we cry for someone to pull us out. We ask firemen to pull us from the burning house and to take us to a place of safety.

We all yearn for someone to save us in the time of need. To be saved means that we are pulled away from a concrete danger and that the ominous threat dissipates. The one who is about to drown longs for a lifeline. Jesus is our lifeline when it seems that we are drowning in the surging waves of our lives—the lifeline we can hold on to.

The second petition is for Jesus to raise us up. He should not simply be with us, as in a storm at sea, sleeping on a cushion:

> But he was in the stern, asleep on the cushion; and they woke him up and said to him, "Teacher, do you not care that we are perishing?" He woke up and rebuked the wind, and said to the sea, "Peace! Be still!" Then the wind ceased, and there was a dead calm. (Mark 4:38-39)

We often experience Jesus sleeping in our boat. We have lost our connection to him. In our hearts we are cut off from him. We are tossed around by the surges and waves of our lives. We have forgotten that Jesus is sleeping in our boat. We long for Jesus to get up and command the storms and surges and waves in and around us to stop. Only then can we survive.

May Jesus no longer delay—that is the third petition. He should not wait so long to come. May he come this very moment. We need him now. This appeal calls out impatiently: May God not linger in his coming, but rather hurry to our side.

Advent is the continuous call for God to enter our lives. May God in his Son Jesus Christ enter our prison, our abandonment, our estrangement, and our fear or depression. We cannot endure any longer. We yearn for him to come and save us.

O Clavis David—O Key of David

> O clavis David, et sceptrum domus Israel; qui áperis, et nemo claudit; claudis, et nemo áperit: veni, et educ vinctum de domo cárceris, sedéntem in ténebris et umbra mortis.

> O Key of David and Scepter of the house of Israel; you open and no one closes; you close and no one opens. Come, and deliver from the chains of prison those who sit in darkness and in the shadow of death.

The fourth O-Antiphon also takes an image from the Old Testament. When God, through the prophet Isaiah, threatens to remove Schebna, the steward of the palace, from power, he promises Eliakim that he will take this office.

> I . . . will clothe him with your robe. . . . and he shall be a father to the inhabitants of Jerusalem and to the house of Judah. I will place on his shoulder the key of the house of David; he shall open, and no one shall shut; he shall shut, and no one shall open. (Isa 22:20-22)

A key had a much more important meaning in ancient times than it does today. Whoever owned a key had powers of control and privilege. He was able to grant or deny entrance into the palace. Back then it was a very large key laid on the shoulders of the gatekeeper. Today we still say that a huge responsibility has been laid on someone's shoulders. It is the responsibility to decide who will be given entrance and who will be shut out.

Eliakim was seen by the church fathers as an image of Jesus Christ. He is not a heartless man who opens the door arbitrarily, but a father to the people. He is an image of Jesus who cares for us like a father or mother.

Jesus is the key of David. He understands that his mission is above all to open those doors that have been closed to us. He looks at those who pound at the door.

When he sees this longing, he opens the door to them so that they can enter the realm of God.

Many Advent and Christmas songs have taken up this image. In these texts either God or Jesus himself opens the door. The song by Nikolas Hermann, from the middle of the 16th century, says: "All Christians praise God upon the highest throne, who today opens up the kingdom of heaven and gives us his Son."

Here it is God himself who opens the door of heaven so that his Son may come down to us. In the final verse of the song, however, it is Jesus who opens the door: "Today he opens the door to paradise; the cherub no longer bars the way. To God be all praise, honor and glory." As a "father" caring for his children, Jesus opens the door to heaven so that even now we can live as if we were in paradise. We can also trust that in death the gate of paradise will stand open for us. An angel will no longer stand in front to keep us from entering.

The key is also an inner image. In fairy tales a key often plays an important role. It usually opens the door to a secret that should be kept hidden. In dreams a key often means that we can enter into our own hearts or into relationship with others.

But sometimes we dream that we are standing in front of a locked door. The key is nowhere to be found. Or the key we want to use to open the door does not fit. Such dreams are meant to warn us to take better care of ourselves. For too long we have lived away from our hearts—and now we can no longer find the way in.

The one who has given up a relationship with her heart will find it difficult to gain an entrance into her inner realm. In such instances this person needs Jesus as a key. It is he who grants us entrance into the inner sanctum of our souls. Through him we reach the foundation of our souls, our true selves. Jesus is also the key to others. He opens our hearts for others as well—not only with the command that we love one another, but also with the fact that in every person we encounter Christ. When Jesus is in our brother or sister, we are not able to close the door to them.

Jesus is the Key of David, the scepter of the House of Israel. He has power over the people, over whom he rules. But his reign is a gentle reign. According to the fourth O-Antiphon, Jesus has the authority to open, and no one can close. He has the power to close, and no power can open.

Such statements make some people afraid. But Jesus is not arbitrary in his use of the key. He has come to open the door to life for us. Only the one who refuses will find the door closed. Jesus does not close the door in order to punish someone. More often it has to do with our living outside ourselves—without a relationship with our hearts. We ourselves can no longer open the door. We ourselves are the ones who have shut it. Jesus can only show us the consequences of a life lived away from one's own heart when we lose the relationship with our hearts and our souls.

In the Book of Revelation John described Jesus as the holy one, the true one,

> who has the key of David, who opens and no one will shut, who shuts and no one opens: I know your works.

Look, I have set before you an open door, which no one is able to shut. I know that you have but little power, and yet you have kept my word and have not denied my name. (Rev 3:7-8)

Jesus says here that he has opened the door, even though the community in Philadelphia did not have much spiritual power. We too can trust that Jesus will open the door if only we try to adhere to his word. Even when we become weak again and again, he will not close the door on us.

On the contrary, we ourselves often close the door to our hearts with our self-accusations. When we make a mistake, we close ourselves off from life. We punish ourselves and believe that we are bad and no longer deserve the grace of God, but the key Jesus holds in his hands is meant to open and not to shut.

The appeal we address to Jesus, the Key of David, is this: O come and open the prison of darkness and the chains of death. This petition describes our situation. We sit in the prison of darkness and are bound by the chains of death. What does that mean? Today many feel trapped, trapped in their fear, trapped in their depression. People who suffer from depression need images to help them understand their experience. They have the feeling of sitting in a dark hole where rays of light cannot enter. When they feel governed by their depression, words of scripture all sound foreign. The faith they carried up to that point seems to have lost its power. May the petition of the fourth O-Antiphon penetrate into this prison of darkness.

What does the image of the chains of death mean? Psychology tells us that the fear of death is essentially human in nature. Even as Christians we feel threatened by the fear of death. But often we suppress this fear by covering it with a thousand activities or by proving our worth to ourselves and to others. Only when we look at our fear of death and hold it out to God will it change. The Advent season is the time to turn to Jesus with our fear of death so that we may free ourselves of this it. We ask that he enter into our fear of death and transform it.

We yearn for Jesus to open the door of our prisons and to break the chains that hold us captive. Advent expresses our longing not to be alone in the prison of our fear, our depression, and our loneliness. We ask that Jesus come and open the door so that he may enter our lives. Then our prison will be transformed into a place of encounter. We ask that Jesus open the door so that we may emerge from our dungeon and cast off the chains that keep us from moving. Only then can we once again openly turn to others.

Suggestions

Dear readers, go through your lives with the images of the root and the key. When you sing an Advent song or sit near the Advent wreath, get a sense of your roots. Maybe you have memories of your parents and grandparents sitting around the Advent wreath and what power they garnered from the rituals surrounding it. When you are quiet, listen within to images of your childhood. It is not so much a matter of escaping into the nostalgia of childhood, but rather, of searching for roots that supported you in childhood.

Imagine for a time the image of a key in your daily life. Listen to your heart and ask yourself: do I have the key to my heart? In my inner house are there rooms that are still locked or that I will not enter because of the darkness or chaos I might find there?

As children we were often afraid to go into the basement. If we look into our inner houses we find rooms that we more or less fear as well. In those places we may also find "intruders" who have broken into our inner lives and taken away feelings of safety and of being at home. Let the image of the key penetrate your inner life so that it may take a place there. Then open up your innermost heart. Now you yourself can find an entrance into your heart. It is also open for Jesus.

One of my Advent rituals is listening to the Advent cantatas of Johann Sebastian Bach. In the cantata, "Now come, Savior of the Gentiles," the bass sings the words from the Book of Revelation:

> Listen! I am standing at the door, knocking; if you hear my voice and open the door, I will come in to you and eat with you, and you with me. (Rev 3:20)

The soprano voice answers this invitation with a heart-felt song:

> Open up, my whole heart, Jesus is coming and moving in.

When I let the music of this cantata penetrate me, my heart opens on its own so that Jesus can move in. This music is full of longing, and it wakes my longing for the one who comes through the door of my heart to be with me and to be one with me forever.

Third Week of Advent

The third week of Advent is about light. In the darkness of our lives, we long for light and inner illumination—we ask that the dark in us may become light.

The third week of Advent features two saints of light, Saint Lucia and Saint Odilia. Lucia is the bearer of light. During the persecutions in Rome she brought food to those in prison. Because she had to do this at night, she put a wreath of candles on her head. Today she is still depicted this way in Scandinavia. Lucia addresses the ancient longing of the northern peoples for light in dark times. But she also represents the human yearning for inner light.

It is said that Saint Odilia was born blind. Then at her baptism she received her eyesight. This story about Odilia reminds us that we are all filled with light at baptism. We ask that the light of faith accompany us in dark times so that we may see everything in Jesus' light. That way it becomes clear what our lives are all about. Faith itself is a light that illuminates us. It allows us to peer through outer appearances into the true nature of all things, where, with the light of faith, we will discover God himself, the God who became human and in whom everything exists and works.

The third week of Advent is about healing. We all long for healing. We feel wounded and hurt by people who do not understand us, who treat us harshly or reject us. Many people feel worn thin in their relationships. They wound each other repeatedly when they are together. Misunderstandings arise, which immediately lead to judgments, put-downs, or rejections of the other. Many cannot find a way out of this cycle of mutual hurt.

The Advent season is a time when we long for healing of our wounds. At Christmas we want to experience family relationships in their wholeness. We hope that the wounds that have come about over the years will not keep us from experiencing respect and peace in our relations with others. We yearn not only for inner healing and wellness in our families but also a restored world where we feel safe and one that feels like our true home.

O Oriens—O Rising Dawn

> O Oriens, splendor lucis ætérnæ, et sol iustítiæ: veni, et illúmina sedéntes in ténebris et umbra mortis.
>
> O Rising Dawn, Radiance of the light eternal and Sun of justice; come, and enlighten those who sit in darkness and in the shadow of death.

The fifth O-Antiphon also offers images of Jesus Christ that can be found in the Old and New Testaments. Jesus is the morning star that rises and announces to us the new day. In Latin we simply have the words, *O Oriens*, "Rising." Luke the Evangelist, in Zacharias's song of praise, speaks of the rising light from on high. In Latin we have *oriens ex alto*. From on high the morning star comes and makes its way over us.

The Second Letter of Peter speaks of the morning star as Lucifer, the bearer of light. The word of the prophets fulfilled in Jesus is:

> A lamp shining in a dark place, until the day dawns and the morning star rises in your hearts. (2 Pet 1:19)

This is a beautiful image. The word of the prophets, which we hear repeatedly during Advent, is like a light shining in a dark place.

The author of the Second Letter of Peter sees our situation as dark and gloomy. We are without hope. We do have the words of the prophets, however, and we should hold onto them until daylight comes. Then Christ himself will rise in our hearts as the true morning star. Christ shines as the bringer of light into our hearts, giving us illuminating insights. Now everything suddenly becomes clear. We are completely in the light. The words of the prophets refer to Christ as light who shines inside us and illuminates all the darkness of our souls.

The image of the "shining of the constant light" refers to the words of the Letter to the Hebrews that are read on Christmas day. Jesus Christ is the refection of God's glory, the image of the eternal and unchanging light, which can no longer be dimmed. In Jesus a clear, unchanging, and undiminished light shines forth, the divine light that also illuminates us and clarifies everything in us that is murky.

We often experience ourselves as murky. Jewish tradition says that we must cleanse ourselves of the murkiness given to us by the father, the mother, and ourselves. We do not see ourselves as we are but rather through the lens of our projections and the projections of our parents, which have clouded our self-image. When the unchanging light of Christ shines within us, it drives away all the murky images that distort our true character. In the radiance of his light we make contact with our true selves.

Another image speaks of the sun of righteousness. This image comes from the prophet Malachi. On the day of divine justice the wicked will be treated like chaff. The arrogant will burn in the fire.

> But for you who revere my name the sun of righteousness shall rise, with healing in its wings. You shall go out leaping like calves from the stall. (Mal 4:2)

These are wonderful images for the day of righteousness. When Jesus is born, the sun of righteousness rises in us, and makes everything right; through it justice flourishes on earth. People will be just with one another, and they will provide for just relations in the world. That will be a day of joy. Like calves we will leap with joy because darkness has been wiped away and the evil-doers no longer oppress us. In the light of the eternal sun we will be filled with joy. This sun of justice, which rises within us in Jesus Christ, is described by the poet Paul Gerhardt in the mid-seventeenth century:

> I lay in the deep night of death.
> You were my sun
> The sun that gave me
> Light, life, happiness and joy.
> O sun, who gave me
> The dear light of faith
> How beautiful are your rays.

The petition of this O-Antiphon is this: "Come and enlighten those who sit in darkness and in the shadow of death." This heartfelt request refers to the Christmas promise of the prophet Isaiah:

> The people who walked in darkness have seen a great light; those who lived in a land of deep darkness—on them light has shined. (Isa 9:2)

Georg Friedrich Handel set this piece to music wonderfully in his oratorio, "The Messiah." In these words the message of Christmas shines forth. The bass expresses the idea of sitting in the shadow of death in circular melodies. Then his voice rises into the heights each time the word "light" is sung, giving expression to human longing for this light.

Luke the evangelist also refers to this passage in the Canticle of Zacharias, when he writes that the radiant brightness from on high will visit us, to give light to those who sit in darkness and in the shadow of death. (Luke 1:79)

This formulation describes a situation we all know: we sit in darkness. Everything around us and in us is dark. We cannot see the light. Our souls are darkened by sadness, pain and depression.

Many feel this way when a loved one has been taken away by death or when a life dream has been shattered. They experience their lives as living in the shadow of death. Death burdens them with its heaviness. They are afraid of the death that awaits them. Or they breathe the smell of death in everything. All is lifeless, meaningless and empty. Everyone who experiences such a darkness in and around themselves cries out with longing that Jesus, the morning star, the sun of justice, and the radiance of uninterrupted light, may fill them with light.

When he illuminates us, everything dark becomes clear and we understand our lives. In the dark time of Advent we yearn for the light that will bring light into our lives so that we can go our ways with confidence.

O Rex Gentium—O King of the Nations

O Rex géntium et desiderátus eárum, lapísque anguláris, qui facis útraque unum: veni, et salva hóminem, quem de limo formásti.

O King of the Gentiles and the Desired of all, you are the cornerstone that binds two into one. Come, and save poor humanity, whom you fashioned out of clay.

In this sixth O-Antiphon Jesus Christ is named King of all nations. The Gospels have already named him the true king. Mathew describes how the wise men from the East come to Jerusalem and ask:

> "Where is the child who has been born king of the Jews? For we observed his star at its rising, and have come to pay him homage." (Matt 2:2)

The wise men from the East recognize the child in the manger as king. They bring him royal gifts. Gold is meant for a king, frankincense for the Son of God, and myrrh for the one who heals our wounds through his death on the cross. Matthew describes the Last Judgment, where Jesus as king separates the sheep from the goats (cf. Matt 25:33f). The Romans had fastened an inscription on the cross to declare his guilt:

> "This is Jesus, the King of the Jews." (Matt 27:37)

Jesus is the king, but completely different from the other kings of the time: He is different especially from King Herod who became terrified when the wise men from the East told him about the newborn King.

John the Evangelist describes the distinctive nature of the kingship of Jesus, especially in his passion account. John transforms the image of king for his times. In the presence of Pilate the governor, Jesus is the truly calm, and thus sovereign, king. To Pilate's question whether or not he is king, Jesus answers:

> "You say that I am a king. For this I was born, and for this I came into the world, to testify to the truth." (John 18:37)

Jesus is not a king who rules over people with power. He is a king who does not allow himself to be hampered by the lies of men. He comes to bear witness to the truth. According to John, a king is the one who knows the depths of the human condition, the one who lives the truth and reveals it. The word "king" here is not a royal term used for a powerful ruler but rather a philosophical or spiritual concept. The king is the wise one ruled by nothing and no one but himself, because he knows the heights and depths of life and he fears nothing.

John also refers to the divine origin of the kingship of Jesus. Jesus says of himself:

> "My kingship is not from this world." (John 18:36)

Because his kingship is not of this world, no worldly king can harm him. Pilate may have him crucified, but he cannot take away his royal dignity for it is not of this world. Similarly, the world has neither power over his kingship nor access to it.

What Jesus said of himself we may also say of ourselves in communion with him. There is a kingship in us that is not of this world. There is a dignity in us that cannot be destroyed by any injury or insult, any violence or oppression. There is something in us that transcends the world and that the world cannot dominate. That is what constitutes true kingship.

In seminars I sometimes have people practice their royal nature in a concrete way. They walk through the room imagining themselves wearing crowns on their heads. While doing this they say to themselves, "I am going through my weaknesses—through situations when I was humiliated or injured, when I had lost all self-confidence." And they repeat to themselves over and over: "My kingship or queenship is not of this world." "When I do this exercise, I will experience in myself a dignity in the midst of instances of injury and degradation, a dignity that no one can take away from me."

When the O-Antiphon calls Jesus the King of the nations, it is saying that he is the true ruler, even if he does not have military might. He rules in his truth and dignity. He has the world in his hands. Those who rule in an external way and hold on to their power are standing on shaky ground. Mary sang in her *Magnificat* that with the birth of Jesus God would reverse every norm in this world:

> "He has brought down the powerful from their thrones, and lifted up the lowly." (Luke 1:52)

This Antiphon says of the king that he is the expectation and longing of the nations or—as the Latin says— he is the *desideratus*. *Desideratus* is related to the word *sidera*, which means the stars. Our longing is turned toward Jesus. We are full of hope that the one who stands above the stars will come to us on earth and that through him our hearts will cling to that star shining on the horizon of our hearts.

Longing means that we reach towards the one who is beyond our needs and desires, the one who can truly fulfill them.

Karl Rahner, the great theologian, has tried to illustrate that, ultimately, in every one of us there is a yearning for the God who became human. Everyone has an inkling that God is not only the one who is above the stars, but also the one who shows himself with a human face. Jesus, the Son of God become human, fulfills the longing that lies deep in the human soul. He is the one sought after by all the nations. Ultimately, all of us are waiting for his coming. Through him our deepest longings for healing, salvation, and freedom are fulfilled.

The king of all nations is described in this O-Antiphon as "the cornerstone that holds the building together." In Latin we have the words, *lapisque angularis, qui facis utraque unum*, or "the cornerstone making both one." In the parable of the evil vineyard tenants Jesus describes himself as the cornerstone:

> Have you not read this scripture: "The stone that the builders rejected has become the cornerstone." (Mark 12:10)

Jesus holds the church building together. He holds our community together. He also holds the house of my life together. He is the ground on which I can build the house of my life. Jesus referred to himself as a rock on which we can build our houses. When we build them upon him, the storms and surges will not bring them to ruin (cf. Matthew 7:24ff).

I am often unable on my own to bring together what is inside me and what is falling apart. Jesus holds my house together. He holds together the opposites in me, and forms a unity of them. Each of us has different opposite poles. We often feel torn between these opposites: between light and darkness, between love and hate, between strength and weakness, between good and evil, between spirit and impulse.

Jesus joins together the polar opposites in me. In me he unifies what I cannot bring together. That is an ancient longing in us: to become unified and not to be torn apart by various ambitions of my body and mind. This is also the longing expressed in the third candle of the Advent wreath: that all three realms that often tangle with each other—belly, heart, and head—may be illuminated in such a way that they themselves become a single light.

The Letter to the Ephesians describes the cross of Jesus as the way to bring together the opposites within us:

> For he is our peace; in his flesh he has made both groups into one and has broken down the dividing wall, that is, the hostility between us. (Eph 2:14)

Through his death on the cross, Jesus brought together not only the Jews and the gentiles but also the opposing forces within us. By his love—poured out for all on the cross—he has brought together the devout and the godless, the spiritual and the secular. The conflicts within us cease. By the love of Jesus on the cross, everything inside us is now touched and permeated and brought together.

The petition of the sixth Antiphon is this: "O come and save the human race, which you fashioned from clay." The Latin reads, *Salva hominem, quem de limo formasti.* Translated literally it means, "heal the people whom you have formed out of clay."

We are formed out of clay and thus we are frail, mortal, wounded. We ask that Jesus may heal us, that he may heal the wounds we have experienced in the course of life. May he also heal the brokenness given to us by our human nature. We are formed out of clay. Jesus heals us by reminding us of our origins in clay and leading us to humility or *humilitas* (formed out of humus soil).

We will only heal if we have the courage to descend into our own earthliness. Jesus heals us by descending from heaven to earth in order to become human. He took on human nature, which is formed from humus soil.

Suggestions

Dear reader, there are three images that you should keep in mind as you make your way through the third week of Advent.

The **first image** is that of light. Pay close attention to darkness and look at the warm light of the candle that burns in the darkness. What does this warm light mean to you? What does it remind you of? What longing wells up when you look into the light?

Next look into yourself, trusting that in the innermost part of your soul there is light. When you look into yourself you encounter not only chaos, darkness and guilt, but also an inner clarity, a well-lit, bright room, a place of peace filled with love.

The **second image** is the cornerstone that holds everything together and unites polar opposites. Ask yourself on what grounds you have built the house of your life. What is the ground you are standing on? What is the basis of your partnership, your family? What is the ground-level consensus that you build upon in your company?

Imagine that Christ is the only ground your house stands on. Christ is the rock upon which you built your house. You did not build it on the sands of illusion but on solid rock, which is ultimately Christ himself. If your house stands on this rock, then, as cornerstone, Christ will hold everything together inside you—even that which you cannot bring together. Wherever you feel torn apart, Christ unites everything so that you can feel truly at home in your house.

The **third image** describes healing, wholeness, a life of well-being and an ideal world. Trust your longing for healing and for a world of well-being as was foretold by the prophets of the Old Testament. Allow these words to stream into you. Then you will come into contact with the healing that lies in the innermost part of your soul.

Each of us has wounded areas of our lives and bodies. Imagine that beyond and below all the hurts and violence there is a room of wholeness and healing. That is where Christ, the true doctor, comes to you and lives with you. That is where you are healthy and whole. That is where no one can hurt you. And that is where the hurtful experiences of your childhood cannot enter. That is where you have remained healthy despite all your wounds.

Fourth Week of Advent

The fourth week of Advent is often very short, and everything is hastening toward Christmas. The image we focus on during this week is the image of Emmanuel, of "God is with us."

At Christmas God comes to be with us forever. At Christmas all the promises of the old covenant are fulfilled. Again and again God pledged both to individuals and to all his people, "I am with you." This pledge now becomes reality. God has bound himself to us forever. He is always with us. Like the mystics, we might also translate this name for God, Emmanuel, as, "God is in us."

God accompanies us. He gave us himself as Jesus in the incarnation. He committed himself completely and utterly to this human being. He is in him. But because God is in Jesus, he is now also in us. That is probably the greatest longing we can experience—that God not only be near us, that he not only intervene for us and accompany us, but that he himself might be in us, that he make his home within us.

O Emmanuel—O Emmanuel, God with Us

> O Emmánuel, rex et légifer noster, exspectátio géntium et salvátor eárum: veni ad salvándum nos, Dómine Deus noster.

> O Emmanuel, our King and Lawgiver, the Expected of nations and their Savior: Come, and save us, O Lord our God.

Emmanuel is a name for God that translates the name Yahweh for daily life. Just as Emmanuel means "God is with us," so too the name Yahweh has the same meaning:

> "I AM WHO I AM" (Exod 3:14)

I am here for you. I am with you. Emmanuel is a statement and an objective description of what God is by revealing himself in the name Yahweh.

Isaiah promises King Ahas, who doubts God's promises, that the virgin will bear a child:

> "the young woman is with child and shall bear a son, and shall name him Immanuel." (Isa 7:14)

Matthew the Evangelist quotes this passage when the angel appears to Joseph in a dream and promises him that Mary will bear a son:

> "you are to name him Jesus, for he will save his people from their sins." (Matt 1:21)

Then Matthew explains this event as the fulfillment of the promise made by the prophet Isaiah:

> All this took place to fulfill what had been spoken by the Lord through the prophet: "Look, the virgin shall conceive and bear a son, and they shall name him Emmanuel," which means, "God is with us." (Matt 1:22-23)

Matthew loves to conceive of the happenings involving Jesus as the fulfillment of Old Testament promises. In Jesus everything referred to in the Old Testament by the divine name *Emmanuel* becomes reality. God is now really with us forever. In Jesus he is with us, accompanies us and shows his solidarity with us. At the end of his gospel, Matthew affirms again that Jesus accompanies us. After the resurrection, Jesus gives his disciples the task to go to all nations to proclaim the gospel. He concludes this command with the pledge:

> "I am with you always, to the end of the age." (Matt 28:20)

Jesus promises the nations that he will be among them for all time through the ministry of his disciples. Whenever two or three gather in his name, he will be in their midst (cf. Matt 18:20). In our prayer together, and in the liturgies, we celebrate, we experience the fulfillment of the promise of Isaiah. Jesus is among us now and in him God himself lives with us.

In this seventh O-Antiphon, *Emmanuel* is the actual sovereign title for Jesus. In addition we are given the titles "king" and "teacher." We have already celebrated Jesus as king in the sixth Antiphon. Now he is also seen as a teacher who demonstrates how our lives may be successful.

Jesus is described as the hope and salvation of the nations. He is the one the people have longed for over the ages—also those in other religions. All of them had the notion that God would fulfill our deepest longings. They anticipated that he would come down to us, accompany us, and share our lives with us. Jesus is also the savior who heals our wounds and fragility, and who mends that which has been torn apart. All of us yearn for this healing. Today many spend a lot of money to protect their health. But no one can guarantee his or her own health. Ultimately it is a gift. We long for the one who will allow us to live healthy lives.

The seventh O-Antiphon closes with a petition that summarizes all other petitions: "O come and save us, our Lord and our God!" In Latin we read again *ad salvandum nos*. That means come to heal us, redeem us, save us, and safeguard us from dangers and demise.

Salvare can mean many things. It relates to the Greek word *sozein* and means "healing," "protection," "saving." Jesus comes to heal our wounds. He saves us from the entanglements of our guilt and also from sinking into the swamps of our lives. He protects our true selves. He protects our inner core, the original image of God within us. He safeguards us from falling apart within, from losing our center that holds everything together. The translation "save us" summarizes what the Latin word *salvare* and the Greek word *sozein* mean. Jesus will help us in our need. He will protect us from sinking in the whirlpools of life. We ask that he might save us from the storms that rage around us.

It is also a longing for protection that is being expressed in the "save us." We yearn to be protected from every wrong turn, from wounds, and from demise. This is a longing for God to fulfill his commitment of *Emmanuel*, that he really be with us when we are in need and that he help us when we can no longer help ourselves.

We direct this appeal for help to the Lord, our God. We speak with him as a loving father: "Come to our aid, our Lord and our God." With the word "Lord," God himself is meant. He is the true Lord and ruler. But "Lord"—in Greek *kyrios*—is also the word for Jesus Christ. The angel announced to the shepherd:

> "to you is born this day in the city of David a Savior, who is the Messiah, the Lord." (Luke 2:11)

In Greek we have the three concepts, *sotér*, *Christos*, and *kyrio*—and in Latin, *salvator*, *Christus*, and *dominus*. "Christos" stands for the promise of the Messiah for whom the people of Israel longed above all else. *Sotér* stands for the longing of the Jews and Greeks for the God who saves and heals—and for a person in whom God allows his holy and healing action to become tangible. *Kyrios* is the title of honor for Jesus. When Jesus is Lord in me, then I will no longer be ruled by my needs, nor by the expectations of others. I am the lord of my own house. I rule myself.

Since Jesus is our Lord, he frees us from all other lords. We become truly free, healthy, and whole. In the last week of Advent, we implore the Lord Jesus to rule in us. There is no harshness in his rule. He is the baby that lies in the manger. He is the one to rule us with his love, and not with external power. We gladly allow a child to rule within us. It brings new life into our hearts, a life that is truly whole, free, and full of love.

Suggestions

Dear reader, let the image of Emmanuel accompany you through the last days of Advent. Imagine: "I am now walking through the city, and God is in fact with me. Jesus is with me." If you know the Jesus Prayer, you can combine this prayer with your breath even in the midst of Christmas excitement. Then you say in the rhythm of your breathing: "Lord Jesus, Son of God, have mercy on me!" Now you notice that you are not alone. This Jesus, Emmanuel, is in you and accompanies you.

This experience transforms your walking. You don't move so frantically. When you go through a snowy forest with the Jesus Prayer, the way you walk changes. You walk consciously. You realize: wherever I look, Christ is there. He permeates the world. He accompanies me on all my paths. He is also in the places I am heading toward. He is the reality that surrounds me always and everywhere.

In thinking about Christmas—about the birth of Jesus in the cave of Bethlehem—you feel that this is a tender God who is with you. The Eastern Church has always imagined the birth of Jesus in a cave, which stands for the middle of the cosmos and for the maternal womb of the earth. When God becomes human, then heaven fertilizes the earth, then the earth takes on God, like a mother's womb. Everything you see now around you is touched, made holy, and healed by the God become human. This world is no longer without God. He is the Emmanuel who accompanies you in all your ways, just as Jesus has promised you. He is also the Emmanuel who is with the cosmos and who permeates the world with his love. The whole world can now become a home for you, dear reader. The world is no longer foreign and distant from God. Everything in you and around you is breathing in God, since God himself became human in Jesus Christ and is now incarnate in this world.

Imagining the Reality
of Christmas Within

Dear reader, I hope that the O-Antiphons, which accompanied you through the Advent season, have prepared you for the mystery of the Christmas. We can only describe the mystery of Christmas in images. The early church often took these images from the Old Testament. In order to describe the extraordinary event of the incarnation, we need such wonderful images as that of the burning thorn bush, the cornerstone that holds everything together, the morning star that announces the new day, the key that opens the door to new life, the roots that make our lives fruitful. The evangelists—I will delve into this further in the next section—described the incarnation of God in images, especially Luke, who according to legend was a painter. With his words he also painted an image: the image of the manger where the newborn child is lying, the image of the angel who surrounds the shepherds with his light, the image of the angel musicians intoning the Christmas song:

> "Glory to God in the highest heaven, and on earth peace among those whom he favors!" (Luke 2:14)

With images that touch the heart, Luke describes what is happening in the incarnation of God. A small child moves the hearts of the rough shepherds. A child lights up the face of the old man Simeon and moves him to sing out in praise:

> "for my eyes have seen your salvation, which you have prepared in the presence of all peoples, a light for revelation to the Gentiles and for glory to your people Israel." (Luke 2:30-32)

Popular piety has carried these images forward. It has also depicted the mystery of Christmas with new images. In the West there is the image of the stall with the manger and with the ox and ass. In the East we have images of the cave and the grotto of the nativity, which also symbolize the center of the world. And there are the many images that various Christmas songs bring to mind.

Dear reader, allow the images of the O-Antiphons to have an effect on you. Those images should root themselves in your heart so that you can celebrate Christmas differently. Ultimately it is not so much a matter of feelings. Through the images of the O-Antiphons and through the images that emerge in the liturgy and in various Christmas cards, the reality of Christmas will form inside you. Christmas will happen inside of you;

God's incarnation will take place in your hearts. Then you will come into contact with the original and extraordinary image that God has made of you. You will experience the peace of Christmas and all that the O-Antiphons have promised: freedom, salvation, healing, and support.

PART 2
Christmas Season

*Biblical Interpretations
of Christmas*

God Becomes One of Us

The feast of Christmas moves people. Even if many today do not understand Christmas as it is proclaimed by our faith, this feast still touches a deep longing that becomes visible behind all the external Christmas busyness. In the media Christmas is valued as a family celebration during which we hope for peace in the world and give gifts to one another. In doing so, we often express the hope that our attitudes toward one another become more peaceful and loving. Christmas is a feast when people open themselves to one another.

But today a deeper understanding of the Christmas feast remains hidden for many. For this reason, I would like in these pages to do an up-to-date interpretation of the biblical texts that are read during the Christmas liturgies. These texts will show us the true meaning of the feast.

We will see that the biblical interpretations touch not only the longings of people two thousand years ago but also what people long for today. It only depends on our willingness to interpret the biblical texts in the context of today's needs. This is what the evangelists did for their times and situations. They wrote about the same events, but they situated their ideas within a different spiritual horizon. Thus it is our task to situate the mystery of Christmas within the horizon of today's thoughts, feelings and hopes.

The Bible does not specify that we should understand the Christmas mystery of the incarnation in a particular way. It shows us many different approaches. It shows us that that God's incarnation has to do with us and that it changes our lives. The Christmas message opens our eyes so that we can look at ourselves and our world with anew.

The incarnation of God shows that God has become one of us. We are no longer alone on earth. God accompanies us on our way. We are also not alone in our limited thinking, our frailness, and our fragility. God became human so that his divine life might flow into us and free us from our mortality and impermanence.

We hear biblical texts but often do not understand them. Or we interpret them in a very specific way. Therefore, it is good to ask the biblical authors what they wanted to tell the people of their day, and what they want to tell us today. Meditating on a biblical interpretation of the Christmas mystery should help us celebrate more consciously from year to year. Then we will understand more and more the true meaning of the feast of the incarnation of God.

Folk piety has interpreted Christmas in a distinct way as a "feast of love." Over the centuries this interpretation has touched the hearts of Christians and non-Christians alike. Folk piety has also addressed basic elements of the Christmas mystery. But for us Christians it is good to venture back to the original texts that interpret the incarnation of God in Jesus Christ. We will see that working with the old texts of the Bible will open up new perspectives for us so that the mystery of Christmas may unfold for us more and more.

Dear reader, I would now like to invite you to focus with me on the Christmas texts of the Bible. Take the days of Christmas—or the time until the 6th of January, the Epiphany—to meditate on the various perspectives that the authors and texts offer for the event of the incarnation of God. A few motifs and themes from O-Antiphons in Advent will appear again in the following pages.

Christmas and the Gospel of Matthew

Matthew the evangelist does not tell us a story of the childhood of Jesus. Matthew is a teacher. He explains the mystery of Jesus Christ by describing it with words from the prophets of the Old Testament. Often the formula appears: All this has happened so that the words of the prophets concerning the Lord may be fulfilled.

Matthew connects the new things that are happening in Jesus with the old words. He is convinced: Every word once spoken by God must become reality, must be fulfilled. In Jesus Christ all the words spoken by God through the prophets are fulfilled.

For us this means that Jesus fulfills the longings that are expressed again and again in folk myths and in all religions. Jesus did not come into the world for us Christians only but rather for all peoples—to fulfill the deepest longings for transformation and the healing of lives.

A New Creation in the Incarnation

The words at the beginning of the Gospel of Matthew remind us of the creation story in the book of Genesis.

In Jesus a new creation begins. In him a new creation is also "unrolled." Creation is renewed when God himself enters the scene. Matthew also places Jesus into the story of God's relationship to Israel. God promises Abraham:

> in you all the families of the earth shall be blessed. (Gen 12:3)

In Jesus this history is fulfilled. In Jesus we are all blessed, and our lives receive a new fruitfulness.

Matthew explains the lineage of Jesus with a genealogy that he develops from Abraham to Jesus. In the genealogy we encounter Matthew's theology. Through the description of the lineage Matthew wants to tell us that God has entered human history through Jesus Christ. He heals this history—not only the history of humankind but also our own personal life stories with all their highs and lows, with their failures, detours, and dead ends.

In his birth Jesus has freed humanity from all its brokenness and has reconnected us with one another. In our history we are no longer simply subject to fate. Jesus himself entered history and he accompanies us through time. Even today miracles of healing can occur through the presence of Jesus—as we were able to experience, for example, in the abolition of apartheid in South Africa, or the fall of the wall dividing Germany in 1989.

Matthew set up the genealogy of Jesus in an artful way. In it there are three times fourteen generations. The

number "three" stands for the three human elements,
head, heart, and belly. Together they comprise a human
being. The number "fourteen" is also the number for
healing. In Babylon fourteen helpful gods were honored.
In the incarnation of Jesus, God himself wants to heal
us through and through.

There are four women specially named in the lineage.
All are foreigners who have come into the genealogy
from the outside. With this, Matthew intends to say not
only that Jesus' message is for all peoples but also that
he accepts all the strange and foreign elements in us.

The four women point towards Mary, the fifth woman.
Like the four other women, she too does not fit into the
family tree. The genealogy focuses on Joseph, not Mary.
But it is said of Mary that she will give birth to Jesus,
the one

who is called the Messiah. (Matt 1:16)

In Mary everything comes to pass that was hinted at
in the other four women. God breaks open the family
tree. They bring anomalies into the well planned se-
quence. Through them we see that God's wonderful
works do not follow human patterns. It becomes clear
that Christ has accepted and brought salvation to history with all its highs and lows, in all its paths and detours. In Mary, God's surprising activity comes to a
climax. Through her, God inserts himself into the history
of salvation and the history of evil in a new way. Here
one can also take a look at the number symbols. Mary

is the fifth of five women who correspond to the five books of Moses—the biblical books of Genesis through Deuteronomy. Five is the number of Venus, the goddess of love. Love completes the law.

Four steps in the stages of life lead from the world of minerals through the world of plants and animals to the world of human beings. But the fifth step is the transition to the divine. In Mary humankind transcends itself and flows into God—by God's becoming human himself. This is a story of triumph and healing in which God himself comes onto the scene, if we only allow his divine life to stream into ours.

The Wisdom of a Successful Life

Matthew the Evangelist invites us at Christmas time to offer to God our life stories with all their ups and downs. We hope that in Jesus divine love will flow into all the events of our lives to heal and transform them. In this way we tune in to our history and come to terms with everything that has happened to us.

In his genealogy Matthew focuses on five stories that tell of the circumstances surrounding the birth of Jesus and the fate of the newborn child. Here again we have the number "five" as an organizing principle. The number "five" refers to the perfection of all people. In Jesus, humankind, having become estranged through sin, will become whole and complete once again.

In his gospel Matthew shapes five great discourses of Jesus—analogous to the five books of Moses in the Old

Testament. We use the word "quint-essence," to mean the epitome or the most essential aspects of something. In his teaching, Jesus proclaims a wisdom that corresponds entirely with the essence of what it means to be human. His wisdom leads us to ourselves and, at the same time, into God. We have become familiar with this wisdom—also from an Old Testament perspective—in the first O-Antiphons.

The wisdom of Jesus brings the wisdom of Moses to completion and connects it with the wisdom of all the nations. This becomes apparent when the magi visit the child Jesus in the manger and acknowledge that the wisdom traditions of east and west, north and south are now joined as one. Jesus is the teacher of wisdom proclaimed in other religions—now summarized and interpreted anew. His wisdom is a wisdom that shows us the way to a successful life.

Matthew sees Jesus as the new Moses. Jesus, like Moses, is the teacher of wisdom. But he is also the liberator who leads us from our prisons into freedom. This is how Matthew presents the history of Jesus' birth against the background of the Old Testament story of Moses.

It begins with Joseph's concern when he learns that Mary is pregnant. In those days extramarital pregnancy resulted in the pregnant woman being stoned to death. Indeed, the law prescribed that the pregnant fiancée was to be stoned. Joseph is an upright man. But he does not follow the law blindly. He combines his justice with mercy. This is an important motif for Matthew.

If Joseph had focused only on the fulfillment of the law, he would have had to give Mary over to be stoned. But he does not want to be just only before the law, but rather before his fellow human beings. He sees that releasing Mary from their engagement is the only possibility—thus doing justice to both the law and to his beloved. Then, during these human deliberations, an angel enters Joseph's dream. The angel interprets the event in a way that Joseph's reason could not comprehend: The child whom his fiancée expects is from the Holy Spirit.

Joseph appears in this dream as a friend of God whom the angel introduces to the mysterious plans of God for his people. The child Mary will bear will be important for all the people. Joseph is challenged to accept Mary as a spouse so that her child might be his son according to Jewish law. The angel frees Joseph from his ruminations, and explains the mystery of the child, who originates in divine creation, in the working of the Holy Spirit. But legally Joseph is made his father, who will give him his name.

Matthew interprets the name Jesus like this:

"he will save his people from their sins." (Matt 1:21)

The word people here means all of humanity, not just Israel. Jesus will free all of humanity from the bonds of sin. An important motif in the Gospel of Matthew is here intoned. Jesus announces not only forgiveness but also empowers humans with the ability to forgive sins. He frees people from the sins they are entangled in, the sins that have separated them from communion with God.

God for All People

In Jesus the messianic promise mentioned earlier is fulfilled:

> "Look, the virgin shall conceive and bear a son, and they shall name him Emmanuel," which means, "God is with us." (Matt 1:23)

Here Matthew is quoting words of the seventh chapter of the prophet Isaiah. In 735 BC the people of Israel were in great danger. In this situation Isaiah the prophet makes King Ahas—who refuses to listen to the word of God—aware of a sign that God himself will give: a young woman will bear a son and will give him the name Emmanuel. In the midst of the difficulties of our lives, God himself intervenes by giving us his Son.

Mary is the "young wife" in Isaiah 7:14, whom Matthew presents as a virgin. She will give us a son, in whom God will create a new beginning for all people. In this context Christmas means that we are never alone in the hardships of our lives. We are not alone—neither in the external crises that shake the world nor in our internal tumults.

According to Matthew, the most important message of Christmas is that God is Emmanuel. He is praised with this title in the seventh O-Antiphon as well. God is with us. He accompanies us through all the hazards that surround us. He never leaves us alone. He descends into our history, which is so often clouded over and threatened by catastrophes. God is with us. When he is with us, catastrophes have no more power over us.

In Jesus God is here for all people. Matthew shows us this by his story of the magi who come from the East to pay homage to the child, to pray to him and bring him gifts. For centuries people have loved the story of the magi from the East. The magi were originally Persian priests, astrologers, or wise men who possessed super-natural knowledge. They saw a star. Astronomers know of the crossing of Jupiter and Saturn in the constellation of Pisces that took place in the year 7 BC. Since Jupiter was the royal star and Saturn the star of Palestine, the Babylonian astrologers realized that a king was being born in Israel. They come to Jerusalem with the question:

> "Where is the child who has been born king of the Jews?" (Matt 2:2)

They identify Jesus with the same word that will be used to designate the crucified at the end of his life. The wise men of the world recognize in Jesus the King of the Jews and pray to him. His own people will hand Jesus over to the Romans precisely because he is their king. Thus he becomes—as he is called in the sixth O-Antiphon—the "King of all Nations."

The magi meet the incumbent King of the Jews, the ruthless tyrant who had had his own sons executed

because he suspected them of treason. The powerful
King Herod is afraid of this child. He is terrified and has
all the high priests and scribes assemble. They must tell
him where the Messiah is to be born. And they answer
him:

> "In Bethlehem of Judea; for so it has been written by the
> prophet: 'And you, Bethlehem, in the land of Judah, are
> by no means least among the rulers of Judah; for from
> you shall come a ruler who is to shepherd my people
> Israel.'" (Matt 2:5-6; cf. Mic 5:1-3)

Matthew is suggesting here that the prophets are fore-
telling Jesus's birth in Bethlehem. They describe his
nature as a "Shepherd of his people." Jesus will be the
Good Shepherd who will gather together his dispersed
people so that they might serve God. As a good shepherd he will pursue the lost sheep of the House of Israel
and will carry it back to God on his shoulders.

The legend centers mostly on the magi as persons,
and paints a picture of their life stories. The legend depicts their road as an image of our pilgrimage. Like the
magi, we too follow the star of our longing. This star
appears at the horizon of our hearts and often leads us
down winding paths as we come to our destination—to
the house where a mother is with her child, where we
can truly be at home.

In the legend, the magi become three kings, one
young, one old, and one with dark skin. All people, with
their differences and inner conflicts, have to set out to

find the child in the manger and pray to him. When the kings pray to the child, they have arrived at the destination of their pilgrimage. They are truly at home, since they have found the way to themselves.

The magi open their treasure chests and give the newborn child gold, frankincense and myrrh. Gold and frankincense refer to the gifts that Isaiah enumerates (cf. Isaiah 60:6). In antiquity all three gifts were also offered up to the sun god as votive offerings. In Jesus Christ the true sun has risen to illuminate the world.

The Church Fathers interpreted the gifts of the magi symbolically. Gold pertains to the child in the manger as the true king. Frankincense refers to his divinity, and myrrh portends his death on the cross.

They can also be images of those gifts that we ourselves are to bring to Jesus. Gold suggests our love, Frankincense our longing, and myrrh the pain and wounds we carry with us. We need not bring only our achievements, but rather we are to bring everything we have to the manger—our love, our longing, and our wounds.

One can also understand the gifts as an expression of wisdom. Gold gilds and transforms us. It makes us royal so that we rule rather than being ruled by others. Frankincense stands for transcendence; there is no wisdom that surpasses God.

Only the wisdom that opens our hearts to God will soothe and heal us: this is what myrrh refers to. As medicinal herb it stands for the healing of our wounds. Myrrh represents the original wisdom of paradise. If we follow it, we will become well.

The flight into Egypt and the killing of the innocents instigated by Herod shows that Matthew is telling of the birth of Jesus as parallel to the birth of Moses. Moses was also saved from the stalking of Pharaoh, who had ordered the killing of all Hebrew male children. Like Moses, Jesus must flee into a foreign land and wait until God brings him back. Matthew interprets this with the words of the prophet:

> This was to fulfill what had been spoken by the Lord through the prophet, "Out of Egypt I have called my son." (Matt 2:15; cf. Hos 11:1)

Jesus is the Son of God. He shows what Israel should be: children of God who rely on God's instruction and who fulfill his will. Like Jesus we should also live as sons and daughters of God. This means for us that we too must depart for a foreign land—for Egypt—to learn the wisdom of the world. It is also a part of our road to study the wisdom of other cultures and religions to discern God's wisdom for us.

Protection for the Divine Child within Us

The divine child who has to go to a foreign land is an archetypal image that appears in many religions. Everywhere we find imperiled divine children: Krishna, Buddha, Perseus, Oedipus, Moses, Siegfried. . . . From endangered divine children always emanates a transformation of the whole world.

The image of a divine child in danger also says something about us. All of us are ultimately endangered divine children. There is something in us that transcends this world and makes us strangers in it. We should not be sad when we sometimes feel like a stranger in this world.

Ultimately we live here in a foreign land. In us there is a longing that transcends this world. In us is the divine child the world cannot handle. When we live as the divine child within us, our surroundings also begin to stir. They react to the divine child within us with the same kind of hostility that King Herod showed. The divine child within us makes people around us fearful. They want to "kill" what is new and unfamiliar so that we do not dismantle their carefully built life edifices.

The angel does not abandon Joseph in the foreign land, but appears to him after some time in a dream and announces that Herod has died. He is told to return. But the angel tells him not to return to Judea. The successor to Herod was said to be just as brutal as the old king. Joseph should move to Galilee instead (cf. Matt 2:19-23). The angel protects the divine child. He guards the endangered boy so that he can develop in safety. That too is an image for us: according to the interpretation of the Christmas Gospel of Matthew, the angel protects the divine child and the wounded child in us. The angel stretches out its arms over us.

The angel guides us towards Galilee. Galilee is ruled by a friendly ruler, but it is a mixed nation where Jews and Gentiles live together. Galilee stands for the mixed country in which our divine child also lives. We live in a world where the devout and the godless are combined, where the non-believing and Christian live next to each other.

The divine child in us does not develop in a world that is healthy and whole, but rather in a world as mixed as Galilee. This is a world where good and evil live together, where healthy and harmful things happen at the same time. In the midst of our daily lives—that are also mixed with success and failure, faith and disbelief, light and darkness—it is our task to allow the divine child within us to develop.

Light and Healing

Matthew shows further on in his gospel how the promises of the prophets are fulfilled in Jesus and in his actions. The promise of the prophet Isaiah—understood by the Christmas liturgy as an interpretation of the Christmas feast—is quoted by Matthew in another place. He tells how Jesus left Nazareth,

> and made his home in Capernaum by the sea, in the territory of Zebulun and Naphtali, so that what had been spoken through the prophet Isaiah might be fulfilled: "Land of Zebulun, land of Naphtali, on the road by the sea, across the Jordan, Galilee of the Gentiles—the people who sat in darkness have seen a great light, and for those who sat in the region and shadow of death light has dawned." (Matt 4:13-16; cf. Isa 8:23, 9:1)

The light of God appears to people who live in the shadow of death not only in the birth of Jesus, but also in the works of Jesus. The light appears to people as Jesus proclaims the word of God. His word is light for their way. It shines into their inner darkness. Thus the fifth O-Antiphon can sing in praise of Jesus: "O Morning Star, splendor of light eternal and sun of righteousness."

Two further passages from the prophet Isaiah describe the works of Jesus. When Jesus heals many who are sick, Matthew says,

> This was to fulfill what had been spoken through the prophet Isaiah, "He took our infirmities and bore our diseases." (Matt 8:17; cf. Isa 53:4)

When Jesus heals the sick he also takes our sufferings upon himself. Later scriptures made a connection between this passage and the death of Jesus on the cross. Matthew refers to it in the context of the healings performed by Jesus.

Another central passage connects Matthew with the healings of Jesus—who asks that these works not be made know to others:

> This was to fulfill what had been spoken through the prophet Isaiah: "Here is my servant, whom I have chosen, my beloved, with whom my soul is well pleased. I will put my Spirit upon him, and he will proclaim justice to the Gentiles. He will not wrangle or cry aloud, nor will anyone hear his voice in the streets. He will not break a bruised reed or quench a smoldering wick until

he brings justice to victory. And in his name the Gentiles
will hope." (Matt 12:17-21; cf. Isa 42:1-4)

These words too belong to the interpretation of what
happened at Christmas. Jesus is born in a hidden place
and his works happen in secret. The powerful are kept
unaware. But the actions of Jesus are a light for us, a
healing light that relieves our sicknesses, and a tender
light that shines quietly into our distress.

When we consider the Christmas story of Matthew
we hear the central message: In Jesus God has entered
into our history to heal it, to pull us away from our
brokenness and to fill us with his divine life. Through
the birth of Jesus we ourselves have become sons and
daughters of God.

We have a divine child in us that is hunted down and
sent into exile like Jesus. We are endangered divine children. But we are not left alone. God is with us. In Jesus
he is Emmanuel who accompanies us through all life
situations—through alienation and homelessness, per-
secution and rejection, misunderstandings and disap-
pointments, injuries and woundedness. When we look
to the child in the manger, we give the ups and downs
of our lives to God's love that has appeared to us in
Jesus Christ.

Christmas and the Gospel of Luke

While Matthew is a typical teacher, a "scribe" who brings forth from his treasury both the old and the new (cf. Matt 13:52), Luke is a gifted storyteller. He unfolds his theology by narrating. And we are woven into his story without noticing it. No one can listen to Luke's wonderful Christmas story without feeling addressed directly.

Most important in Luke are the proclamation scenes. His message unfolds in these scenes. They tell us how to react—or how not to react—in response to the Christmas message.

The Angel's Proclamation to Zechariah (Luke 1:5-25)

The first proclamation scene tells us how we should not react. The angel Gabriel announces to the old priest Zacharias in the temple that his wife Elizabeth will bear him a son. But Zechariah has doubts. He has enough rational reasons to push away the angel's quiet encouragements. Then the angel takes away his ability of speech so that he may become open to what God has in store for him.

Not only does Zechariah need to become quieter outwardly, he also has to quiet down his rational deliberations. Otherwise the angel won't have a chance to announce to him something new coming from God. The angel leads Zechariah into a place of quiet—not only to prevent him from saying anything, but also to quiet the thoughts with which he continually evaluates himself and his wife. The place of quiet is free of judgments. Here Zechariah is transformed. At the birth of the child, he is able to speak once again.

In order to understand the message of Christmas we also need quiet. We need to quiet our prejudices and the reasons for our resistance, for our closing ourselves off from the gentle encouragements that touch our souls, especially at Christmas.

With all the rational arguments against the angel's message quieted, Zechariah opens himself to the mystery of Christmas. When he can speak again, he grasps what is happening at Christmas. He extols it in the song of the *Benedictus*, which the church sings every morning at Morning Prayer. Zechariah understands that God visits us in the incarnation of his son.

God's visiting humankind is also a favorite motif of Greek myths and many fairy tales. God is coming for a visit. But people turn God way. We also need to prepare in quiet so that will not reject God at Christmas. Then we can sing with Zechariah:

> "By the tender mercy of our God, the dawn from on high will break upon us, to give light to those who sit in darkness and in the shadow of death, to guide our feet into the way of peace." (Luke 1:78-79)

The Angel's Annunciation to Mary (Luke 1:26-38)

Zechariah—the old man and the priest—reacts to the proclamation of the angel Gabriel with doubt. Mary, the young woman, the simple girl from Nazareth, believes the angel. Both poles are within us in their contrariness—doubt and faith. Luke invites us to trust more in the pole of faith.

Mary has found grace with God. He delights in her and thus gives her his loving care. The angel's pledge to Mary also applies to us. God is delighted with us. But often we do not react.

Mary surrenders herself to God's grace:

> "Here am I, the servant of the Lord; let it be with me according to your word." (Luke 1:38)

Mary is shown here as a representative of the people Israel. While Israel rejected God's will, she will fulfill it as a representative of the people. In this passage Luke shows us how much he appreciates Mary as a woman. In contrast to the man Zechariah, she allows herself to be affected by the word of God and to trust God. Because she trusts in the word of God, the people will find salvation.

Action emanates from God. But it also depends on people's decisions whether or not they allow God to act in their lives. Mary makes room for the action of God in her personal life. That has repercussions for all humankind.

Luke describes Mary as the original image and model of faith. Mary believes in the angel. But she is frightened at the angel's words. She does not close herself off, however, but rather considers what the angel wants to tell her. The angel announces to her that she will conceive a son who will be called the

"Son of the Most High." (Luke 1:32)

"The Most High" is a favorite designation for God. The angel explains to Mary how she will conceive:

"The Holy Spirit will come upon you, and the power of the Most High will overshadow you." (Luke 1:35)

The Holy Spirit himself will impregnate the virgin. This not only explains the virgin birth of Jesus but also serves as an image for our lives. The deepest fruits we can bring do not come from ourselves nor from others but rather are brought about by the Holy Spirit. In this scene, Mary, the woman of faith, is a model for all Christians.

We ask God to create new things in us through his Holy Spirit. We, therefore, should not think too little of ourselves. Like Mary we should trust in God's ability to work great things in us and from us. In the gospel we hear:

> "For nothing will be impossible with God." (Luke 1:37)

From the original Greek text we hear, literally, "For not powerless for God is each word that he says." When God utters something, then this too has power. It brings about what it declares.

True faith consists in our trusting the word of God and not setting limits on God. For God nothing is impossible. He chooses Mary, an insignificant girl from Nazareth, in order to make the impossible possible in the world.

He also chooses us in our very weaknesses and limitations to bring about his work of healing in this world. Christ desires to take on a form in us. The prerequisite is that we say like Mary:

> "Here am I, the servant of the Lord; let it be with me according to your word." (Luke 1:38)

The Meeting of Mary and Elizabeth (Luke 1:39-56)

Before Luke describes the birth of John and the birth of Jesus, he tells us the beautiful story of the meeting between Mary and Elizabeth. With this story he connects the birth of John with that of Jesus and then he interprets the events for us. Mary is the woman blessed above all other women. For she carries God himself inside her.

Luke tells us a wonderful story about two people meeting. A twelve- or fourteen-year-old girl gets up and makes her way through the mountains. This journey normally takes about four days. Mary must have been a confident woman to have trusted herself with this journey. Her experience of God in the Annunciation sets her in motion.

Elizabeth too is set in motion. When Mary greets her, the child leaps in Elizabeth's womb. She comes in contact with her fruitfulness and with the new being that is growing within her. And she is filled with the Holy Spirit. She becomes a prophetess who recognizes in Mary the mystery of her motherhood.

This wonderful story is not only about what happened back then. The scene is an ancient image of every deep human encounter. Every meeting has to do with discovering the mystery of Christ in others. When we understand this, then the child in us leaps up. We discover the mystery of the other as well as our own mystery. We come into contact with the child in us.

Like Mary, we too need to get up and get on the road so that such a meeting might be possible. We have to use our own feet to arrive at someone else's home. We need to cross the mountains—the mountains of inhibitions and prejudices—in order to see the other person the way he or she is. At Christmas we hope that we meet each other with more love than usual. The meeting of Mary and Elizabeth is a model for our encounters at Christmas—in our families and with friends and acquaintances.

Elizabeth calls Mary holy because she

> believed that there would be a fulfillment of what was
> spoken to her by the Lord. (Luke 1:45)

Elizabeth sees in Mary the one who believes. She is a model for our faith that God will also fulfill for us all those things he has promised to us. He will also accomplish great things for us if we, like Mary, trust in his words.

Mary answers Elizabeth's blessing with a song of praise, what we call the *Magnificat*. Luke formulates it in such a way that it can be our song as well:

> I acclaim the greatness of the Lord,
> I delight in God my Savior,
> who regarded my humble state.
> Truly from this day on
> all ages will call me blest.
>
> For God, wonderful in power,
> has used that strength for me.
> Holy the name of the Lord!
> whose mercy embraces the faithful,
> one generation to the next.
>
> The mighty arm of God
> scatters the proud in their conceit,
> pulls tyrants from their thrones,
> and raises up the humble.
> The Lord fills the starving
> and lets the rich go hungry.

God rescues lowly Israel,
recalling the promise of mercy,
the promise made to our ancestors,
to Abraham's heirs for ever.

In the *Magnificat* Mary interprets what she experienced in the Annunciation and what will be accomplished in the birth of Jesus.

Mary is the representative of Israel, but also the voice of all the poor and disenfranchised who receive new benefits in the birth of Jesus. In Jesus' birth, God removes the mighty from their thrones and raises up the poor.

Liberation theology has rediscovered in the *Magnificat* a song of hope for the poor. Feminist theologians see in it a song of liberation for women. Both movements capture important aspects of the gospel. Luke is an advocate for the poor and for women as well. All people can sing this song for themselves and with it praise God who has done great things for them. Here we find the idea that God upsets all of our standards, raising even the lowly parts within us and satisfying our deepest hungers.

The Birth of Jesus (Luke 2:1-20)

There is hardly a person who is not touched by the story of the birth of Jesus, as told to us by Luke. Luke weaves together three different stories: the story of the census, the birth of Jesus, and the announcement of the birth to the shepherds.

Luke not only quotes historical facts; he also interprets them. He places the birth in the political world of the Roman Emperor Augustus in order to show that Jesus is the true king of peace. For Luke, Augustus does not bring well-being as some contemporary inscriptions say of him. Jesus does, the one born as a poor child in a stable.

The birth of Jesus in an insignificant corner of Palestine carries a salutary meaning for the whole world. Jesus is the true Savior and Lord. It is he who brings true peace—not Augustus, who had himself celebrated as the emperor of peace. With his story, Luke criticizes not only the political ideology of the emperor but also the political theology of the resistance movement of the Zealots, who rebelled against the census. Mary and Joseph obeyed the orders of the emperor. The overthrow of relationships does not happen by force, but rather from the inside outwards.

In Jesus, God enters this story. The peace, which appears through Jesus in history, has historical and political effects. According to Luke, Christians should bring the peace of Christ into the whole world. Mary and Joseph made their way to Bethlehem.

> While they were there, the time came for her to deliver her child. And she gave birth to her firstborn son and wrapped him in bands of cloth, and laid him in a manger, because there was no place for them in the inn. (Luke 2:6-7)

The inn where there is no place for the couple refers to a room in a private home where travelers could stay overnight. But there was no room in this home. So Mary and Joseph had to go to the cave underneath the house, where there was a feeding trough carved out of the rock. Jesus is born in a place of utter poverty. In this birth in the poorest surroundings, Luke sees the fulfillment of God's promises to his people.

The third scene—the announcement to the shepherds—is for Luke the most important. Here he gives more detail than in the other proclamation scenes. This depiction with the shepherds has to do with us as well— the angel announces the Christmas message to us. We in turn should act like the shepherds. We too should keep the night watch so that we do not lull ourselves into illusions and sleep away our lives. We should open ourselves and endure our own nighttime, so that it becomes not a dark night but rather a sacred night—a Christmas night.

An angel steps toward the shepherds and God's glory appears with the angel and shines upon them. The night, the darkness of human hearts, is transformed by God's light. The angel announces a great joy to the shepherds. Here Luke uses the Greek word, *euangelizomai*. It is good tidings, glad tidings that the angel proclaims not only to the shepherds, but to us.

The proclamation goes like this:

> "to you is born this day in the city of David a Savior, who is the Messiah, the Lord." (Luke 2:11)

Luke uses three terms to explain the mystery of Jesus. I want now to explore these three terms in more detail, terms that I have already addressed briefly with regard to the O-Antiphons and that affected Jewish and Greek imaginations in a similar way.

In the Old Testament, the Greek word *sotér* (savior) refers to the action of God. In the Greco-Roman world, emperors, philosophers and doctors were given this name. For example, Emperor August was referred to as savior. But Jesus surpassed all these human saviors. Jesus saves us from danger and he pulls us from the swamps of depression when they threaten to pull us down.

Doctors are also saviors. Martin Luther correctly translated *sotér* with the word *Heiland* (savior-healer). Jesus heals our hurts and our wounds. He preserves our true essence and protects our innermost core.

Jesus is not only savior but also the *Messiah*, the Christ, the Anointed One of God. The true savior is the Messiah who emerges from Judaism and fulfills the promises of God. He frees his people from oppression and slavery. Jesus leads his people out of their own personal and collective Egypts—out of imprisonment into the Promised Land given to the people as their own possession. Jesus also leads us out of our inner imprisonments, out of the compulsions of our fears and our perfectionisms, into freedom and thus into the land where we truly live instead of "being lived."

The third term is *kyrios*, which is translated as "Lord." The Greeks used *kyrios* for the emperor. In the Old Testament, God is the true Lord. Jesus comes from God and he is God's son. But he is also the Lord who brings peace and well-being to the whole world—in fact, in a more lasting way than any other ruler can. When Jesus rules in us we become free. We are no longer ruled by our needs and passions but rather we rule over ourselves. We are also no longer ruled by people and their expectations and opinions. We are truly free. By artfully combining these three terms with each other, Luke describes the mystery of the incarnation of God in Jesus Christ. He does not speculate, but rather expresses who this Jesus is by means of a story. We would rather hear stories than reflect on theological discussions about the God-Jesus relationship, discussions that are often incomprehensible. In this moving story about the birth of Jesus, we can intuit the mystery of this man. He is completely man, but he comes from God. He is the savior the whole world longs for.

In his narrative Luke combines heaven and earth, human longing and divine action. In the way that Luke tells of the birth of Jesus, he brings about the joy in us that is proclaimed by the angel. The divine is made visible and understandable through human words.

In the proclamation to the shepherds, the word "today" appears for the first time. Luke will use the word seven times in his gospel. The event back then in the fields of Bethlehem is happening for us today when we read the Gospel of Luke. We have a part *today* in the drama Luke describes for us. We look at the image painted for us. And by looking we become one with what we see.

We become eyewitnesses of what has happened and spectators to the divine drama when the words to the shepherds are proclaimed in the liturgy and when we find our way into the events of the liturgy. We are transformed in the spectacle and then return home as people who are changed. Luke speaks the word "today" to our longing. Today everything should happen to us that happened to the shepherds in times past. Today our longings will be fulfilled.

Next to the angel of the proclamation there appears an entire host of angels, who praise and extol God:

> "Glory to God in the highest heaven, and on earth peace among those whom he favors!" (Luke 2:14)

Through the birth of Jesus, heaven and earth are joined together. God's glory appears on high. And in Jesus, God's peace appears below, on earth.

This is a paradox. A child is born in a stable and God's glory lights up the heavens. Peace is the reflection of God's glory on earth. The Greek word for peace, *eirene*, means not only the elimination of wars and clashes, but also the well-being that God brings to us. The Hebrew word for peace, *shalom*, stands for the original condition of all people. In the birth of Jesus, God reestablishes humankind as it was meant to be.

The Greek word, *eirene*, also means tranquility, the quiet of the soul. When God becomes human, people with their restless hearts can experience peace; their longings are fulfilled. *Eirene* refers to the harmony in which everything comes to agreement. In the birth of Jesus, God and people, earth and heaven experience a new consonance. There is harmony between God and humankind, spirit and matter, between angels and people. This peace, tranquility, and harmony are awarded to people with whom God is well pleased. *Eudokia* means the delight of God and the loving movement of God toward his people. It expresses divine benevolence toward humankind. In Jesus Christ, God has shown us his love in order to call forth a reciprocal love from us.

Eudokia expresses that God has always been in a relationship with humankind and that God wants to deepen this relationship through the birth of his Son. The *eudokia*, the tender benevolence of God toward us, is made visible in the child in the manger.

There is no one—no matter how hardened—who would not be transformed at the sight of a child, who would not let his hardened face break into a smile. This is how God's human heart and tenderness are revealed to all of us in this gentle child.

At the angels' hymn of praise, the shepherds rise in order to see the child in the manger. They also want us to get up so that we, with our hearts ready, will hurry to the manger to see what God proclaims to us at Christmas. The shepherds and Mary are models for our faith. In faith we respond to God's visiting humankind in the birth of Jesus.

The shepherds see the child and the manger and understand what the angel had promised them. They tell what they heard from the angel. Mary answers in her own way to their words:

> But Mary treasured all these words and pondered them in her heart. (Luke 2:19)

In Greek we have the word *synterein*. This means that Mary understood the words she heard together with the events in the manger and in her own life. This is our task as well. We too should bring together everything heard and seen at Christmas in our lives.

Mary's second reaction is referred to in Greek as *symballein*, a tossing together. Mary tosses the various thoughts, words, and sights back and forth in her heart. She tries to understand what has happened. She not only wants to ponder these things intellectually, but also to feel what has happened to her and what is being transformed in her life as a result.

This is how we too should contemplate the story of the birth of Jesus in our hearts. We should move the story back and forth until our feelings settle—into the mystery of the divine love that has invaded history and appeared visibly to us all.

Simeon and Anna (Luke 2:21-39)

The shepherds and Mary are not the only ones who are models for the faith-filled acceptance of the Son of God, Jesus Christ. Luke, the storyteller, uses another important motif loved by both the Greeks and the Jews—the old man who experiences yet one more special event in his life.

Luke loves meetings between people that God himself initiates. In such meetings the mystery of God is made tangible for us. For Luke, the Greek, it is always meetings with men and women. Both experience the event together and recognize God's work in it.

But it's not only the polarity between man and woman that becomes important in this story. It's also the contrast between law and gospel, joy and suffering, being raised up and the pain that Jesus will cause his mother. It is not a world of well-being that awaits Mary. The joy about her son, the Anointed One of God, is mixed with pain over the fate he will suffer. Here Luke is showing the contrasting experience within our own souls. We too experience God as the one who brings joy to our hearts but also the incomprehensible one who calls forth contradictions in us and expects a painful transformation from us.

Mary and Joseph fulfill the Law of Moses by bringing the child to Jerusalem to consecrate him to the Lord. But the law is only a transition to the grace of God that has appeared in Christ. In the midst of the ritual something astonishing happens—the meeting of Simeon and Anna. The old man holds the child in his arms and extols the mystery of the child:

> "for my eyes have seen your salvation, which you have prepared in the presence of all peoples, a light for revelation to the Gentiles and for glory to your people Israel." (Luke 2:30-32)

With this hymn Luke interprets—in the figure of Simeon—the Christmas event. The child, whom Simeon holds in his arms, is the salvation longed for by the faithful of Israel. He is the light who enlightens the Gentiles. The Christmas event is meant not only for the Jews but for the whole world. For the people of Israel the birth of Jesus means glory. Jesus imparts a new dignity to Israel, the people from whom the Messiah and Savior will emerge. But Israel does not have an exclusive claim on him. He is here for people of all religions the world over, to brighten their eyes and fulfill their longing.

As in the hymn, Luke depicts the contradiction in Simeon's heart—but also in our hearts. Jesus is joy and light, but also sword and suffering. A sword will pierce Mary, who will share in the sufferings of Jesus. Jesus brings not only salvation but judgment as well. Through him human thoughts are revealed. Through him is made visible how people close themselves off from God.

In this tension between light and suffering, Luke hints that he is writing not only a simple story, but also a tragedy in the Greek sense. In Greek tragedy one also gets the sense that, through the varied emotions in the play, the feelings and emotions of humankind are evoked and addressed.

Anna appears next to Simeon. While Simeon is described as a faithful and just man, Anna is called a prophetess. Man alone does not represent faith as Luke understands it. A woman must always be juxtaposed with him, a woman who brings to expression another aspect of what it means to accept Jesus in faith.

Luke describes the man as just and faith-filled. He sheds light on the woman's character by describing the story of her life and her current activity. This is the art of the storyteller who alternates between description and telling.

Anna has lived through all three phases of womanhood—virgin, spouse and widow. She is a woman who prays, spending significant time in the temple. She sees more deeply and glimpses what God is doing in Jesus, in whom the salvation longed for by faithful Israelites has become a reality for all people. Through him humankind is freed from its imprisonment and alienation. We are now free people, just as God had envisioned for us in his creation.

The Twelve-Year-Old Jesus in the Temple (Luke 1:40-52)

After the encounters with Simeon and Anna, Mary and Joseph return with Jesus from Jerusalem, back to their daily lives in Nazareth.

> The child grew and became strong, filled with wisdom; and the favor of God was upon him. (Luke 2:40)

Luke loves the word *charis*. He uses the Greek word for "grace" with its Greek connotations:

> *charis* is something which brings joy. . . . *charis* is charm, attraction, 'grace', something that makes a pleasant impression. . . . it is a matter of the enjoyable and attractive impression made by elegance, beauty and charm. In this sense *charis* is the expression of a typically Greek view of life. (Edward Schillebeeckx, *Christ: the Experience of Jesus as Lord*, trans. John Bowden [New York: Crossroad, 1981], 102.)

As a growing child, Jesus gratifies others because of his wisdom and pleasant bearing, because of his beauty and grace. But after giving us this ideal image of Jesus as a growing child, Luke introduces the opposite aspect. Jesus is not the loving and low-maintenance child. In the story of the twelve-year-old in the temple, Luke depicts the first family conflict. Jesus wants to be independent. He does not return with his parents from Jerusalem. When they find him after three days of unsuccessful searching, he is sitting among the teachers, listening to them and asking them questions (cf. Luke 2:46).

In Mary's words we sense an accusation and the pain her son has caused her:

> Child, why have you treated us like this? Look, your father and I have been searching for you in great anxiety. (Luke 2:48)

Jesus' answer is incomprehensible to his parents. He calls God his father. He belongs to God, not to his parents. This is the first time in Luke's gospel that Jesus speaks of God as his father. His parents have to accept this distancing of their child. Luke is not depicting a harmonious family, but rather a family with the conflicts we all know— suffering from children's growing differences, the painful letting go of children, the inability to make sense of their life paths. But after Luke's depiction of this conflict of puberty, he offers an ideal image once again:

> And Jesus increased in wisdom and in years, and in divine and human favor. (Luke 2:52)

The ideal and reality alternate. Both poles belong to Jesus; both poles belong to us as well. Only in the tension between closeness and distance, understanding and confusion, community and alienation do we grow into the figure that is pleasing to God and that corresponds to our inner beauty (*charis*).

Luke uses an artful narrative to place before our eyes the story of the birth of Jesus. In the few remarks I have made I would like to arouse curiosity about Luke, this gifted author. He addresses both Jewish and Greek readers in the same way. With his words, he touches—beyond all religious and cultural traditions—people's hearts and awakes in them a premonition about the mystery of God. He never overdoes it. He has a fine feel for each situation he depicts. He tells his story in such a way that we can sense his deeper meaning. He offers us these images cautiously and with restraint so that we can perceive through them the depths of the divine mystery. We never tire of these images. In each situation, new aspects of divine love emerge, if we give ourselves to the story of the birth and childhood of Jesus in Luke.

Luke shows us, in his descriptions of the persons surrounding the divine child in the manger, how we should react to the mystery of Christmas. Like Zechariah, we should quiet ourselves in order to be open to what is new at Christmas. Like Mary we should give ourselves over to the quiet impulses the angel awakes in us again and again. And we should allow the word of God to be realized in such a way that something new can be born in us, and so that we can come into deeper contact with God's original image of us.

Like Mary we should connect the external events—and the events in our hearts—with the words of the Bible. Then the mystery of Christmas will transform our lives. Simeon and Anna want to open our eyes so that we see the light of God in the small child in the manger. In this way we can recognize in our daily lives those moments when the divine light becomes bright in our darkness, and illuminates everything in us and around us.

Christmas and the Gospel of John

John interprets the mystery of Christmas in the prologue at the beginning of his Gospel. He assumes that incarnation of God cannot be narrated nor can it be expressed in purely theological language. One can only sing a song about it—a hymn that extols the incarnation in images. In the prologue hymn, the essence of Johannine theology emerges. What John extols in the prologue, he then describes in his gospel with the use of images.

The Light Came into the World

The prologue of the Gospel of John is perhaps the most beautiful Christian hymn about the incarnation that we have. In it the mystery of the incarnation is described:

In the beginning was the Word. (John 1:1)

With this verse John follows the origin of Jesus back into the depths of the Godhead. Here the phrase "In the beginning" of the creation story in the book of Genesis finds an echo. If in the beginning was the Word, it means that all of creation is literally permeated by the Word of God, making it understandable for us. Creation itself is already a revelation of the glory of God. In it God expresses himself for us; in it God shows us his glory. Creation is God's first word. In it is proclaimed the Word that becomes human in Jesus. We cannot look to Jesus without bringing creation into view as well.

in him was life (John 1:4)

In John, life and death are the central opposition. The question is, "How we can really live?" Many people live merely on the surface. For them life consists only of working and eating, enjoyment and variety. But for John such a life has the same meaning as death.

True life is only possible in God and from God. The yearning for life—for eternal life, for a quality life—is just as strong today as at the time of John. What is a well-lived life? John shows us that only in God can we become fully alive human beings. God himself gives life; in him is life itself.

The experience of God has always been the experience of one's own vitality. For John, life is a streaming forth. He always uses the image of a spring from which water bubbles forth offering a continuous freshness. Ultimately it is the source of God himself, from which our human life flows, fructifying us and the world. Light and darkness are—next to life and death—the other opposition in John. Many people grope in the darkness, living on without meaning. But life and light belong together. Genuine life emerges from right insights. When I see myself and the world as they really are, I am able to live in the right way.

Light makes the world bright. It enables me to see, to perceive and to understand myself and my life. Seeing means not simply groping around in the dark, but discerning a way to perceive myself. Light means the glory in which I am not afraid and in which I can get my bearings. That is why the appeal of the fifth O-Antiphon is "Come and enlighten those who dwell in darkness and the shadow of death."

Jesus is the true light that comes into the world. At Christmas we celebrate, in the birth of Jesus, the illumination of our human darkness by a divine light. In the dark recesses of our human souls Jesus wants his light to shine bright so that we ourselves have the courage to illuminate the whole truth of our souls.

Light wants to illuminate us. It is the goal of every spiritual path. People yearn for inner light today as well. They want to look behind the scenes, to get to the bottom of things, to understand and see clearly. May the curtain hiding everything rise so that we see reality as it is, so that we can live in the light. As long as we live in darkness, we do not understand ourselves. We go astray and lose ourselves.

> He came to what was his own, and his own people did not accept him. (John 1:11)

In Jesus the true light came into the world. But here we sense that many have not accepted him. Even his own, the ones who belong to the chosen people, have not accepted him, but reject him.

> But to all who received him, who believed in his name, he gave power to become children of God, who were born, not of blood or of the will of the flesh or of the will of man, but of God. (John 1:12-13)

Whoever accepts Christ will be created anew and born of God. They no longer define themselves by the world's expectations, by their life stories, or by their parents. Blood no longer plays a role. It is no longer a matter of natural talent, ancestry, or family history. They do not receive their existence from the will of the flesh, or merely human procreation. In the acceptance of the Word, we are not only children of our parents, but also children of God. In God we are free of the influence of parents and of the world. We no longer define ourselves by the judgment of people, but by our relationship to God. To be born of God is the true dignity of human-kind. This dignity frees us from all entanglements in human relationships.

The hymn climaxes with the Word:

> And the Word became flesh and lived among us. (John 1:14)

In this line lies the gist of the Gospel of John. The One who was completely God entered the realm of the earthly and the frail and became completely human. He became flesh.

Flesh is the image of that which is bound to the earth, of that which is frail, transitory and helpless. It symbolizes the nothingness of human existence. Having a home—or more precisely a tent—reminds us of the temple, where God's glory is made present among us. The Word-made-flesh replaces the temple; it is the place of the undisguised presence of God in the world. The image of a tent reminds us that, for Jesus, this world is not a place that lasts. Jesus was in this world only temporarily. Now he is again in the glory of God.

The Greek word used here for "living in a tent," *eskenosen*, has the same letters as the Hebrew word *schekina*, which describes God's living among his people. It means the healing and liberating presence of God in the world. What happened back then has changed the world forever. From that point on, God wants to take on flesh in each one of us. The most essential aspect of this reality is addressed:

> we have seen his glory, the glory as of a father's only son (John 1:14)

We see glory in this person, Jesus of Nazareth. John is not developing a theology here, but rather he is speaking about an experience that he and others had with this person Jesus. "Beholding glory" has something to do with contemplation. The Latin *contemplari* means "to look." Here the mystical character of the Gospel of John finds expression. By looking at the person of Jesus, I am illuminated by the glory of God. I behold his beauty in the flesh and in the historical person of Jesus. In Jesus' living in the world, in his actions and discourses, God's glory is radiant.

The revelation is also veiled. When I look contemplatively at Jesus, I am more and more transformed into that glory that God intended for me as his son and daughter. Looking does something to me. It brings me into contact with my true and undistorted image.

The Gospel of John wants to answer the question of how we can behold God's glory in the flesh—in the concrete person of Jesus Christ. This is not a beholding with the natural eyes of the body but a looking with eyes of faith. Faith consists in beholding God in the flesh of Jesus.

The glory of the only Son of the Father is "full of grace and truth." With this expression John reminds us of the appearance of Yahweh on Sinai. God appeared to Moses as the one who was rich in grace and truth. In Jesus, God leans graciously and tenderly towards us, his people.

The Greek word, *charis*, which is translated as "grace," originally meant an action or behavior that causes joy and makes one happy. In Jesus God prepares for us unutterable joy that can no longer be taken away from us. In him he bestows on us his tender love. In Jesus God's reliability and fidelity toward us are made tangible.

John translates the Hebrew word for fidelity with the Greek word, *aletheia*, which we render in English as "truth." In Greek, "truth" means that the veil covering and distorting reality has been pulled back. *Aletheia* indicates divine reality. In Jesus the veil that obscures the essence of human existence is taken away. In him we now perceive who we really are. In Jesus we realize our origins. And in him we recognize God, the source of all being, the original ground of our human existence.

Buddhists say, "Truth is." It is simply there. It is undistorted reality. Jesus wants to open our eyes so that we might perceive the world as it is, so that we might recognize divine reality in it and in each person, for every person reflects God's countenance. And in creation God himself shines forth, if we take away the veil that covers everything. The mystery of contemplation consists in looking behind the veil. The fruition of our lives depends on it.

> No one has ever seen God. It is God the only Son, who is close to the Father's heart, who has made him known. (John 1:18)

The hymn comes to its climax in this cry of exaltation. None of us can see God. Even Moses did not really see him—only his back (cf. Exod 33:18-25).

Jesus is the only one who has truly seen God, for he himself is God.

He rests at the Father's heart. He is in a most intimate relationship with the Father. He revealed God to us and made him visible to us. In Jesus we behold God in his everlasting love. In him we are taken along into intimacy with the Father. In Jesus, we too rest at the heart of the Father. This is how our lives are illuminated.

When we look at Christmas through the lens of the prologue to John's gospel, we find the following: By beholding the child in the manger, we are filled with the light and love of God. We behold in this child the glory of God. But Christmas also means that we are able to look at ourselves and people around us with different eyes. God's glory also shines forth in them. God has become human and as a result has filled everyone with his light.

Christmas is not only a mystical event between us and God, but also a challenge to see ourselves with different eyes and to encounter one another in a new way. The incarnation of God is the reason why we yearn at Christmastime to accept each other with love and to live with one another in peace.

Heaven's Ladder and the Marriage Feast at Cana

The mystery of Christmas is visible not only in John's prologue. It also shines through in the images that pervade his gospel. I would like to focus on two images that should make Christmas even more accessible to us.

One is that of heaven's ladder. John describes how the disciples gradually find their way to Jesus. In all of their callings it is a matter of seeing. The disciples must come and see how and where Jesus lives. In Jesus they will see God's glory. Jesus himself alludes to this seeing:

> "Very truly, I tell you, you will see heaven opened and the angels of God ascending and descending upon the Son of Man." (John 1:51)

In the spiritual tradition, Jacob's ladder, in the Old Testament, was always seen as an image for contemplation. What Jacob saw in his time is fulfilled in Jesus Christ, in whom heaven opens above our eyes. In him we recognize the connection between heaven and earth, between God and humankind. In this way we are blessed—as Jacob once was.

Jesus wants to lead us into the mystery of God. Thus the image of ladder becomes a key to how we should read the gospel. At Christmas, heaven opens and angels climb up and down between God and us. Christmas is the fulfillment of God's promise to Jacob:

> "Know that I am with you and will keep you wherever you go, and will bring you back to this land; for I will not leave you until I have done what I have promised you." (Gen 28:15)

Christmas is the promise that our lives will be fruitful. God will accompany us on our paths until we arrive in the land he has promised us. In this land we are truly ourselves, and like Jesus we will become light through and through.

After the calling of the apostles, John shows us in another image what the mystery of Christmas means for us. In the story of the marriage feast at Cana, John wants to reveal more than Jesus' enjoyment of going to weddings and celebrating with others. Everything reported in this story has a symbolic meaning. It begins with the introduction:

On the third day there was a marriage in Cana of Galilee, and the mother of Jesus was there. (John 2:1)

John has introduced passages with the words "the
next day" three times since John the Baptist appeared
on the scene (1:29, 35, 43). Thus the third day, after the
four days John wrote about, is the Sabbath. On that day
creation is completed. The marriage feast at Cana describes the mystery of the incarnation of God in Jesus
Christ. In Jesus, people will be re-made into the people
originally intended to be part of God's creation. At the
same time, the third day reminds us of the day of resurrection. In the resurrection of Jesus, our lives are transformed and filled with divine wine. In Jesus, God
celebrates the marriage between himself and his people.
Just as a man and a woman join themselves to each
other, so also people become one with God in the incarnation and resurrection of Jesus.

For the crowd, the wine has run out. They want to
celebrate the wedding feast. But they aren't able to. They
don't have any more love. They are incapable of love.
This is the poverty of humanity. For John it is not so
much a matter of being delivered from guilt, but of
being freed from the inability to love. There are only six
stone water jars in Cana. Six is the number of incom-
pleteness. People's lives are incomplete. We have work,
troubles and vexations. The stone jars symbolize that
our lives are stony. The water in these jars is meant for
cleaning. But the true cleansing happens, not with old
rituals, but rather with the incarnation of Jesus, for in

the incarnation God has purified his people and returned them to their original beauty.

The mother of Jesus was also at the wedding. In John's gospel Mary has an important role at the beginning of Jesus' public life, and then only at the end, beneath the cross. Here too a deep symbolism becomes visible. The mother of Jesus initiates the miracle of the transubstantiation. She made possible the miracle of the incarnation by giving birth to her son. She is the gateway through which Jesus steps toward people. She introduces him to humankind.

Mary is the first one to notice the shortage. She points out to Jesus that the wine has run out. Jesus seems to address his mother in a very standoffish way.

> "Woman, what concern is that to you and to me? My hour has not yet come." (John 2:4)

In this passage John is not depicting the personal relationship of Jesus to his mother. It has more to do with Jesus' reservation about the miracle of the wine. He believes his hour has not yet come. His hour is the time of glorification on the cross and in the resurrection. When his hour has come, only then does he give wine abundantly.

Jesus himself is the wine that gladdens the human heart. In the hour of death he will open his heart for us. Then we will be able to drink the wine that will stream from his heart. The true wine is the love of God that comes from the heart of Jesus. Mary too understands

Jesus' answer at the wedding feast at Cana not as a refusal. She already believes in Jesus' transformative love before he gives a sign in the miracle of the wine. The apostles believe only after the miracle (cf. John 2:11).

Christmas means—according to this image of the wedding at Cana—that God is celebrating his wedding with us in the incarnation of his Son. Here our lives take on a new flavor—the sweet flavor of wine. In our bodies we sense not only air and blood circulating, but also the love of God flowing through us. That is reason enough to celebrate and to enjoy with one another the new taste of our lives. This is how we should celebrate and enjoy the new life and the new love that fills us, both in the Eucharist and in festive meals with our families.

In the early church the gospel passage of the wedding feast at Cana was read on the feast of the Epiphany on January 6, along with the story of the journey of the wise men to the manger. With this wedding story the church apparently was responding to the pagan rite of the cult of Dionysus and giving it a Christian "baptism." On the vigil of the feast of Dionysus—the night between the 5th and 6th of January—three empty jars were set up in the temple in Elis, in the northwestern part of the Peloponnese peninsula. In the morning they were full of wine.

The early church saw in Jesus the fulfillment of the Dionysian longing for ecstasy, intoxication, and transformation. Jesus is not an ascetic like John the Baptist, who preaches only renunciation. He brings the fullness of life. He gives us a new taste. Dionysus was also the god of love and sexuality. What people long for in sexuality and in love is fulfilled in Jesus. In him God's love has become not only visible and tangible but also drinkable. God's love gives our lives a new and intoxicating taste. Jesus does not stand in contrast to Dionysus—as Nietzsche saw it—but rather, he is the fulfillment of Dionysus and of the longing for ecstasy he represents.

Friedrich Hölderlin was justified in trying to see Dionysus and Jesus together, to connect the longing for ecstatic love with the longing for contemplation in which God's glory flows into the hearts of people. Christmas is the feast when the love of God permeates us and brings us into a similar ecstatic mood to that of the cult of Dionysus. But we do not need to get drunk. Instead we celebrate the transformation caused by a divine love that gladdens our hearts like wine.

Christmas in the Letter to Titus

During Christmas Midnight Mass a wonderful passage from the letter to Titus is read:

> the goodness and loving kindness of God our Savior appeared. (Titus 3:4)

The Letter to Titus describes the mystery of Christmas in images and concepts understandable to the Greeks. He translates the Christmas message for those who get very little from romantic images—those who want to know what they can rely on and how they might best live their lives.

Philanthropia, God's love for people, was an important ideal for Greek philosophy. God's love for humankind was made visible in the child in the manger. The Latins translated *philanthropia* with *humanitas dei*, with "the humanity of God." With this they set a different tone. In Jesus the true human being has appeared, the original and unblemished face of humanity shines forth for us in Jesus Christ—a true epiphany.

In ancient times, epiphany was an important concept that described either the sudden appearance of a deity on earth, or the appearance of the emperor. Whenever the emperor visited a city, one spoke of an epiphany. It often led to the emperor's bestowing special graces on the city, such as amnesty for prisoners or the lowering of taxes. In contrast to these worldly benefits, we now have God's goodness and benevolence as they appear in Jesus. In this epiphany God frees us from our inner compulsions. In the incarnation, God himself bestows his loving grace on us. This grace heals and transforms us.

Sotér, "savior," was an important concept for the Greeks. To save means to make healthy and whole. The greatest distress for the Greeks was the experience of inner brokenness. In Jesus God makes us whole. He creates us anew, he binds together in us what has been broken by wrong ways of living.

In Jesus God saves us from ruin. People experienced the world back then as corrupt, ruined and lost. Antiquity was on its way out. Whatever was valid earlier had lost its validity. One could no longer count on law and order. Everything was falling apart. In this lost world the birth of Jesus is the promise that God is offering us a new beginning. In Jesus, the savior, God's grace is made visible so that we are now able to become true human beings. The world today also yearns for the true image of humanity to shine forth. If this happens, the world will heal, it will experience well-being, it will be saved.

The Letter to Titus has another wonderful passage where he talks about the appearance of Jesus. This too is read at Midnight Mass. But here the author connects the mystery of the incarnation of God in Jesus Christ with Jesus' task as educator, as *paidagogos*.

Jesus is the great pedagogue. He guides us to true life. He leads us out of false models of living and disease-causing dependencies so that our lives may flourish. We see this in the words:

> For the grace of God has appeared, bringing salvation to all, training us to renounce impiety and worldly passions, and in the present age to live lives that are self-controlled, upright, and godly, while we wait for the blessed hope and the manifestation of the glory of our great God and Savior, Jesus Christ. (Titus 2:11-13)

The liberating and saving grace of God has appeared in Jesus Christ. The epiphany is the invasion of the divine into this world. In Jesus God himself has entered into the world. He became visible in order to save and to heal us. This saving happens in our being led to a new and worthy life.

Jesus heals us by leading us to lives reflecting our true essence. Pedagogy is an important value in Greek culture. An educated soul makes a person happy. The Greek philosophers strove to educate people so that the image of God would be imprinted in them and would reflect their true essence. In the Letter to Titus, Jesus is the great pedagogue who fulfills the longing of the Greeks for true humanistic education.

The beginning of this education involves the renunciation of godlessness and worldly desires. Godlessness does not mean the kind of atheism that believes there is no God, but rather an attitude of irreverence before God, an attitude that nothing is holy. The Church Fathers considered among the worldly appetites the typical enjoyments of antiquity, such as circus performances, horse racing, and processions with pagan idols in decline. The early Christians saw these stimulating entertainments as signs of decadence and lack of feeling for human dignity. These entertainments offered only a voyeuristic display and consumption of violence, sexuality, and sensationalism. They were an expression of a way of life that leads to corruption and keeps people from living in their divine dignity. The age of television and internet is like antiquity in decline. Today too there are people who live their lives only as spectators instead of really living.

The life Jesus wants to educate us for consists of sober-mindedness, justice, and devotion. These are three of the Greek cardinal virtues which people need for a fruitful life. Instead of the fourth virtue, fortitude, the author speaks of waiting "for the blessed fulfillment of our hope." Apparently waiting for the fulfillment of our hope in the arrival of Jesus Christ enables in Christians a life of courage with which they can stand up to present hardships.

Christians—according to the Letter of Titus—demonstrate by their prudent (wise), just (correct, suitable), and devout (divinely informed) lives that they have gone to the school of the great Savior and Redeemer Jesus Christ, and that they allow themselves to be directed by the spirit of Jesus. The well-being that the birth of Jesus brings is expressed in a behavior that corresponds to the ideal image of Greek philosophy. In the way Christians live, the well-being and healing of people through Jesus Christ becomes visible and tangible.

That is a challenge for us today as well. Do people see by our way of life that we live by means of a different and divine source and that we are free from greed and addictions? Christmas calls for a Christian culture and a way of living that shine forth in this world.

At Christmas in 1939 the mortally sick Catholic philosopher and Nazi opponent Peter Wust answered his students' questions about the most important message of Christmas by saying, *"Apparuit benignitas et humanitas Salvatoris nostril Dei"*—"The goodness and benevolence of God, our Savior, has appeared." In contrast to the distortion of the human image in National Socialism, Peter Wust looks to the image of the true person who has appeared in Jesus Christ.

This is the important message the Christmas feast wants to announce to us today as well: In Jesus we see the true human being. We should take this image into ourselves more and more so that we will be transformed into it. This would be beneficial not only for us but for our society as well. So many false images of humanity are propagated, that we long for the true person. We long for love for humanity as it has appeared in Jesus Christ—and as it wants to appear today once again.

Christmas in the
Letter to the Hebrews

In the main liturgy at Christmas, the message at the beginning of Letter to the Hebrews is proclaimed. In it we hear that God has spoken through the prophets again and again, but now he speaks to humankind through his Son. Then the author describes the essence and task of the Son. He is the Son that God

> appointed heir of all things, through whom he also created the worlds. He is the reflection of God's glory and the exact imprint of God's very being, and he sustains all things by his powerful word. When he had made purification for sins, he sat down at the right hand of the Majesty on high. (Heb 1:2-3)

In these sentences the author expresses aspects similar to those developed by John in his prologue. Through the Son, God created the world. The Son is a reflection of the glory of God. The Church Fathers interpreted this image in this way: Jesus is light from the light of God.

He reflects God's glory in this world. And he bears the stamp of God's nature.

Here the image of a stamp is used, something that makes a copy from something original. Just as the impression bears the characteristics of the embossing stamp, so too does Jesus mirror the nature of God. In him we recognize God. At the same time, God uses the human nature of Jesus as a seal so that his nature can become visible to humankind in this world. Jesus now radiates God's light and glory in this world.

It is not the nature of the Son simply to be the reflection and likeness of God, but rather he carries the universe with his powerful word. At the same time, he holds the world together by his word, which is full of power. The incarnate Son is the guarantee that the world will not fall apart, but endure. In Christmas the world receives a new dimension. It no longer diverges, but rather has a bond that holds it together—Christ, the Son of God, who has come into creation to heal it and to keep it safe. Thus the incarnation in the Letter to the Hebrews also has a cosmic meaning.

After this description of Christ's nature, the author tells what Jesus has done for us, his people. Jesus' work consists in purifying us of our sins. He washes them away so that they no longer adhere to us. This liberating image is taken from the purification rituals known by all religions. Jesus has wiped away sins once and for all. They no longer stick to us. He completed this work with his death on the cross.

Jesus then sits at the right hand of God. He, the incarnate Son of God, is now our advocate, who intercedes for us. We humans now have someone from our midst with God to champion our concerns before God. The work of Jesus continues in his intercession for us.

One from our midst is with God and represents us. This gives the reader of the Letter to the Hebrews new courage. The author wants to instill courage in the Christian who is tired in faith by giving us a new and uplifting view of Jesus. A glance toward the one who is with God should liberate us from the burdens, life paradigms, and feelings of resignation that we carry around with us:

> let us run with perseverance the race that is set before us, looking to Jesus the pioneer and perfecter of our faith, who for the sake of the joy that was set before him endured the cross, disregarding its shame, and has taken his seat at the right hand of the throne of God. (Heb 12:1-2)

A glimpse at the Son, who ran the life race with success and perseverance, and now sits on the victor's throne, should inspire us to continue with our battle. Jesus is the initiator, the leader in faith. He takes the lead in faith, completes it, and brings it to its goal. A glance toward Jesus should strengthen our faith so that our lives too will be successful. We will run the race of life with eagerness, and reach our goal safely and joyfully with Jesus' help.

We celebrate Christmas in the spirit of the Letter to the Hebrews when we look at our world with new eyes. That is especially true of creation. Nature has been transformed through the incarnation of God. We can now see everywhere in creation the reflection of God's glory.

Jesus has entered creation so that it no longer stands in opposition to us (as we sometimes experience in natural catastrophes), but rather as the place where we meet God himself. Jesus is the one in whom God speaks to us today. Christmas means listening to the voice of God: what does he want to tell me today through his Son Jesus Christ? For the Letter to the Hebrews, the word Jesus proclaims is always a word of trust, hope and assurance. These words benefit us when so many other kinds of words are spoken.

The Inexhaustible Mystery
of Christmas

In the second half of this book we have reflected on the interpretation of Christmas by five authors of the New Testament. We have asked ourselves what the ancient texts might have to say to us today. The five different interpretations have shown us that we can observe Christmas using different approaches. Not every perspective will be adequate for each person. But the variety of interpretations allows us to trust in what our hearts want to tell us each Christmas.

Sometimes we are drawn to the familiar texts of the Gospel of Luke. These remind us the most of the Christmas feasts we celebrated as children. We hear Luke's text in Johann Sebastian Bach's Christmas oratorio. Many Christmas songs echo Luke's words as well.

But sometimes we are in the mood for other interpretations. With Matthew we understand Christmas as the healing of our life stories. Or with John we want to meditate our way into the inexhaustible mystery of the incarnation of God.

I personally know several approaches to the mysteries of Christmas. I read the biblical texts. I listen to Bach's Christmas oratorio and the Christmas part of "The Messiah," by Georg Friedrich Handel, who interprets Christmas by using Old Testament texts. That is also an interesting way to understand Christmas. Or I look at Christmas paintings created by artists over the past thousand years and I meditate my way into the interpretations of the Christmas event that I find in them.

But then I ask again and again with John, what does it really mean that God became human? How do I understand myself and the world, if it is true that God has entered into this world and has bound himself to it forever? I try not only to satisfy my intellect but to look deep into my soul. What kinds of inklings about Christmas arise in my soul? And I connect these inklings with the words of the Gospel of John.

The Letter to Titus tells me that God's love of humanity has appeared in Jesus. When I read the farewell letter of Peter Wust to his students, the relevance of this text occurs to me. Then I see Christmas not only through the lens of the Letter to Titus but also through the eyes of the philosopher who searched honestly for the right image of humanity in a troubled time, and who wrestled for his faith.

If at Christmas I walk through nature and meditate my way into it—whether it is still green, or covered with white snow and grown quiet—then the message of the Letter to the Hebrews is important. The incarnation touches and transforms the whole world. Everywhere

I go I meet Jesus Christ who has stamped the reflection of God's glory into nature. We can never meditate enough on the incarnation of God in Jesus Christ. New ways of looking emerge again and again.

A mystery is by definition inexhaustible. The mystery of Christmas is inexhaustible. Even if I have preached often and written books about Christmas, the mystery never ends. Again and again I ask, "What does it mean that God has become human, that God has entered our history as a child? How can I understand that God has become one of us, that God has taken on a human face and has become visible as a person?"

The five biblical authors we have looked at in this book proclaim the message of Christmas within different horizons. They address different audiences with differing perspectives. They address their longings. Christmas fulfills our longings for security and home, for happiness and fruitfulness in life, for light, and a love that transforms our broken love. Christmas fulfills our yearning for a new beginning. Christmas helps us let go of the past and devote ourselves to the future with a new vitality. For we are no longer left to our own devices. God himself has entered our history and has inaugurated a new beginning with us. God accompanies us. He is Emmanuel, God with us.

Thus Christmas accompanies us throughout the year. At Christmas we celebrate what we can confidently confess each day of the year: I am not alone. God is with me. God is in me. His divine life, his divine love is in me and is transforming my life.